Speak to My Heart, GOD

KAY ARTHUR

HARVEST HOUSE PUBLISHERS
Eugene, Oregon 97402

Cover by Koechel Peterson & Associates, Minneapolis, Minnesota

SPEAK TO MY HEART, GOD
(Formerly titled *His Imprint, My Expression*)
Copyright © 1993 by Kay Arthur
Published by Harvest House Publishers
Eugene, Oregon, 97402

Library of Congress Cataloging-in-Publication Data
Arthur, Kay, 1933–
    [His imprint, my expression]
    Speak to my heart, God / Kay Arthur.
        p.cm.
    Originally published: His imprint, my expression, 1993.
    ISBN 0-7369-0773-4
    1. Meditations. I. Title
BV4832.3 .A78 2002
242—dc21   2001051702

Printed in the United States of America.

04   05   06   07   08   09   / BP-CF /   10   9   8   7

To my firstborn...
who was the hidden sorrow,
the seed of many "if onlys,"
but who now belongs
to the Lord and warms
my heart with his
care and love...

The story of your salvation is in
these pages...May it bring
hope to many who
wonder if their prodigal
will ever come home...

Contents

Words of Trust

Words of Grace

We know that God causes all things to work together for good to those who love God, to those who are called according to His purpose. For those whom He foreknew, He also predestined to become conformed to the image of His Son, so that He would be the firstborn among many brethren; and these whom He predestined, He also called; and these whom He called, He also justified; and these whom He justified, He also glorified.

ROMANS 8:28-30

Words of
FAITH

When You Wonder
If Life Has Any Purpose

Why was I born? What is the purpose of my existence? What am I worth to God?

Have you ever asked yourself these questions? I have. In fact, I was considering all this just the other day as I sat in my big old chair (where I often pray), worshiping our Father by rehearsing aloud all that He is and has done. As I did, my mind went to the amazing truths of Ephesians 1. I thought of the magnificence and power of our Father in creating the world and in forming man from the dust of the earth. Then I thought of Ephesians 1:4:

"He chose us in Him before the foundation of the world!"

Awesome, isn't it? To think that even before God created the heavens and the earth, He knew you and me, and He chose us!

Following this, my mind went to the fact that God has the course of history all planned out. God's plan wasn't broadsided by Satan in the Garden when that evil deceiver tempted Adam and Eve

11

to sin. Everything was already in place, for Jesus was already the Lamb of God, slain before the foundation of the world. And so I began to thank our Father for making "known to us the mystery of His will," and for "the administration of the mystery...hidden in God" for all these ages (Ephesians 1:9-10; 3:9-10).

God has a plan, and neither man nor the devil can thwart it.

Then my mind went on to Ephesians 2:10 where He tells us that before the foundation of the world our Father prepared the good works that we are to walk in! Talk about understanding our worth! Talk about knowing that our lives have a purpose!

Do you know this truth, my friend? And are you living in the light of it?

Do you realize how absolutely precious you are to God? Do you realize the significance of your life? It has a purpose. A specific purpose! As Ephesians 1:11 says, we live "according to His purpose"—and His purpose is always the very best!

You are not an accident! You are not useless. You are not worthless. You are not unredeemable. Your worth and purpose in this life do not depend on who you are, on what you have done, or on what has been done to you. Your worth and purpose do not depend on where you have been, even if you have been to the very precipice of hell.

Your worth and purpose depend on God and God alone—His will, His calling, His choosing, His love.

> *"He chose us in Him before the foundation of the world, that we would be holy and blameless before Him. In love He predestined us to adoption...through Jesus Christ to Himself, according to the kind intention of His will" (Ephesians 1:4-5).*

God paid the dearest of prices to redeem you from your life of sin and independence from Him. You were dead in your trespasses and sins; you were condemned to death row for all eternity. And justly so because of your sin. Yet the Father gave His Son to die in your place by the most brutal of deaths. He did this when you were still walking your own way, not even realizing the price He was paying. And had you known it, you probably wouldn't even have cared! That's how lost you were!

God loved you when you were His enemy. When you were a sinner, ungodly, and without hope, He loved you, pursued you, and wooed you. And He did not let go until you gave in and succumbed to His desire to be your Father, your God, your Lord, your Master, your Redeemer (read Romans 5).

Have you begun to comprehend the breadth, length, height, and depth of Christ's love for you, a love that surpasses knowledge (Ephesians 3:14-21)? Or are you walking around, lost in the maze of the enemy's lies? Are you blocked at every turn by thoughts and feelings that lead you down dead-end paths? Are you confused, not knowing where to go, where to turn, or what to do because you are being led by your own emotions, your own feelings, your own suppositions? Or are you living by the evaluations, the opinions, the counsel of others rather than by the absolute truth of God's inerrant Word?

Our peace, our happiness, our well-being, our soundness of mind, our effectiveness all go back to what we believe—and *whom* we believe.

It does not matter what you experience, what you feel, what you think or hear. If it does not agree with the Word of God, then it is a lie and has its origin with the great deceiver, the father of lies (John 8:44).

Don't miss the knowledge of your worth and your purpose in this life by believing his lies. Choose to believe God, no matter what.

Ultimately, then, it comes down to: *Where will you put your faith?* In the character of God, in the Word of God, or in a lie? You alone can decide that. It's up to you. This is the choice God gives you. And no one can decide for you.

Everything you are going through, all that you are dealing with, has one ultimate purpose: that you may know the love of God and live in the light of His extravagant and more-than-adequate grace, which has been poured out on you. That is what you were born for: an intimate relationship with God. That is the purpose of your existence. That is what you are worth to Him.

But this intimate relationship requires two things: First, that you set aside time so your heavenly Father can communicate with you through His Word and through His Spirit. Second, that you spend time communicating with Him in prayer.

If you want intimacy with God your Father, then you will have to make the time for it. And if you realize that it must be your highest priority, then nothing will stop you.

When nothing stops you and you put yourself in the position for God to meet with you, you will find that everything else falls into proper perspective because you know His voice when He says, "This is the way, walk in it." And you'll walk in confidence, knowing without a shadow of a doubt that you are

> *"His workmanship, created in Christ Jesus for good works, which God prepared beforehand so that we would walk in them"* (Ephesians 2:10).

My Response to His Words...

When You Feel Out of Focus

Deep down inside, are you dissatisfied...or even downright miserable?

Most of the world feels that way at one time or another—even those who seem to have everything that should make them happy. Unfortunately, this also includes many Christians.

Have you ever wondered why? Especially here on the North American continent where we live in a land of plenty. No nation has greater access to Christian literature and teaching and programming than we do. And currently, at least, no other body of Christians has as much religious freedom as do the Christians in North America.

Yet for all our freedom, for all our resources, we are hurting, miserable, and relatively impotent. We are ignorant of the "power which is in us."

As I sat meditating on the first week's study in Henry Blackaby and Claude King's *Experiencing God,* the statement "The focus needs to be on *God*, not on *life*," caught my attention. Suddenly it all clicked into place: Misery comes when *we* are the focus of our lives.

Reason with me for a moment.

Where is much of the emphasis in the world today? Isn't it on "self"? That is certainly the focus in our society, with self-esteem, self-fulfillment, self-actualization....But think about the emphasis in much of our Christian teaching, books, seminars, radio, and television. Isn't it also on *self?*

And what is this focus accomplishing? Are the majority of Christians any happier? Any more productive? Walking in greater power? Are they being used of God to impact their society? Statistics tell us *no!*

However, when God becomes the focus, rather than self, then everything takes second place to His will for our lives. In essence, nothing else really matters. He is the only One whom we have to please. He is the only One to whom we are truly and rightly answerable.

And we need not fear that such an attitude—the focus of pleasing God alone—will make us hard, unloving, or uncaring. If our center is God, then what He works out in our lives will reflect His character, His likeness.

When we are set free from the bondage of pleasing others (including self)—of currying others' favor and others' approval—then others (and self) will not be able to make us miserable or dissatisfied, for only what pleases God will please us.

If we know we have pleased God, then, like Paul and Silas, we can sing in the prisons of life, for we know our sovereign God holds the key, and He can open the prison doors whenever He pleases! After all, He is God; He rules over all. God does as He pleases in heaven and on earth. Nothing can stay His hand, and no one can say to Him, "What have You done?" (Daniel 4:34-35). The will of God will never be thwarted.

The wonderful benefit of all this is that if you make the will of God your focus day by day, if you seek to please Him alone, then you'll find yourself satisfied with life. Misery will slip away like a whipped puppy with its tail between its legs. Life will take on purpose.

God will meet you right where you are—not demanding or expecting you to live by the standards of others or of the world, nor according to the talents and gifts of others. Rather, you will simply live by His power, which will work in you and lead you into the good works He ordained for you before the very foundation of the world (Ephesians 1:19; 3:20; 2:10).

The will of God for your life is simply that you submit yourself to Him each day and say, "Father, Your will for today is mine. Your pleasure for today is mine. Your work for today is mine. I trust You to be God. You lead me today and I will follow."

Take one day at a time. "Tomorrow will care for itself," for He is God over all your tomorrows (Matthew 6:34). Therefore, you can "commit your way to the LORD, trust also in Him, and He will do it" (Psalm 37:5).

> *Gracious and holy Father, give me wisdom to perceive You; intelligence to fathom You; patience to wait for You; eyes to behold You; a heart to meditate upon You; and a life to proclaim You, through the power of the Spirit of Jesus Christ, our Lord.*
>
> BENEDICT

My Response to His Words...

When You're Suddenly Shaken

Have you ever been doing just great, and then someone says something, or you see something, or you remember something from the past, and suddenly your peace is gone?

Suddenly you feel like a failure. You wonder why you've done what you have done, or why you haven't done more, or why you haven't done things differently.

As you begin to think about it all, a cloud of depression blocks out the warmth and contentment you felt just moments ago.

That happened to me one day when our youngest son, David, came home from college for the weekend. On Sunday afternoon, when he was ready to leave to return to school, he came to say good-bye to me. I had been taking a nap, and David came in and kissed me good-bye.

When he left, I prayed for him and his safe journey, then rolled over to catch another "forty winks." But as I did, impulsively my thoughts raced to the attic of my mind to pull out dusty boxes of stored memories. I began rehearsing days gone by, searching them out to see if I had been the mother I should have been—if I had adequately prepared my son for what lay ahead of him in life.

As I rummaged through the past, suddenly *if onlys* and *what ifs* began to attack me. And just like that, the peace and contentment that had been mine when I lay down for a nap were gone. What had happened?

Nothing had changed...except my thoughts!

Yet that was enough to change the entire atmosphere of my afternoon.

My joy had turned to mourning—my peace to turmoil. My rejoicing over recent spiritual victories was now overshadowed by doubts, inadequacies, and fears. Not because of anything my son had done. David is a fine young man—stable, confident, committed. But because of my own mental turmoil—because of a thought process.

And, Beloved, you know I'm not unique. You, too, have been there. And, if you are like me, it probably has not been a one-time occurrence, but something that can come upon you when you least expect it.

Why? Where do these thoughts come from? And what do we do when this happens?

The problem is that so often we forget that we are in warfare and that Satan's target is our mind. Because "as [a man] thinketh in his heart, so is he," it is only logical that Satan would attack our mind (Proverbs 23:7a KJV). He disguises himself, of course; he doesn't want us to think he has anything at all to do with this evil thought process. Yet he does. And that is why God tells us to take up

> *"the shield of faith with which you will be able to extinguish all the flaming arrows of the evil one. And take the helmet of salvation, and the sword of the Spirit, which is the word of God" (Ephesians 6:16-17).*

This was precisely what I had to do that Sunday afternoon after David left. I had to purposefully choose to bring every thought captive to the obedience of Jesus Christ (2 Corinthians 10:3-6) and to "Philippians 4:8" it at the door of my mind. Then I had to walk by faith—taking truths such as Romans 8:28-30 and living by them rather than by my feelings, thoughts, and evaluations of life.

How am I able to do this? How am I prepared to do this? What have I done to make me victorious in these times of mental warfare?

The answer is: I know our God and His ways.

To have this knowledge, two things must be an integral part of my life; I cannot survive without them: regular, diligent study of the Word of God, and a consistent quiet time alone with Him. Without these two basic pieces of spiritual equipment, we cannot withstand Satan's assaults on our mind.

Time alone with God and faithful study of His Word equip and establish us so we can stand firm when Satan attacks our thoughts.

> *"Brethren, whatever is true, whatever is honorable, whatever is right, whatever is pure, whatever is lovely, whatever is of good repute, if there is any excellence and if anything worthy of praise, dwell on these things. The things you have learned and received and heard and seen in me, practice these things, and the God of peace will be with you" (Philippians 4:8-9).*

MY RESPONSE TO HIS WORDS...

My Response to His Words...

When You're Dealing with What Ifs

Are you prepared to see Jesus?

Suppose, just suppose, that you knew the coming of the Lord Jesus Christ was near.

Suppose that you had inside information that your time "to occupy until He comes" was about over.

Suppose, just suppose, you knew for certain that by this time next year you would be standing—as an individual—before your God and your Lord, having to give an account of how you have lived as His child (Romans 14:10-12; 2 Corinthians 5:10).

Would it make a difference in the way you live today? Next month? During the coming year?

Well, we don't know about next year, but we do know that the Lord Jesus Christ will return someday—"in the twinkling of an eye" (1 Corinthians 15:52).

And from all that God's Word has to say about the end times…from all that we see going on in our world…and from the prompting of the Spirit of God, we feel that we need to order our days before our God accordingly.

God has told us to redeem the time because the days are evil and to live as if His coming is imminent. And He has told us that we will be held accountable to Him for the way we live as His children.

Let me share with you just some of the things for which God's Word tells us we shall be held accountable.

We shall be held accountable for...

- what we have been given (Matthew 25:1-30)
- what we know (Luke 12:4-48)
- our stewardship of God's Word (1 Corinthians 4:1-5)
- what we teach others (James 3:1; 1 Corinthians 3:10-15)
- our giving (Philippians 4:14-17)
- our words (Matthew 12:36-37)
- our leadership (Hebrews 13:17)

Now, follow this five-step plan as you look at the days ahead.

First, go through this list, look up the Scriptures, and ask God to search your heart in each area in the light of His Word.

Second, set some specific goals for your life. For instance, since you are accountable to God for knowing His will and for doing it, you need to plan how you are going to make the time to be alone with Him in His Word so that He can speak to you.

Third, as you set these goals, formulate definite plans to reach them. For instance, to follow through on the example used above (making time to be alone with God), schedule your day to allow yourself uninterrupted time to be alone with Him.

Fourth, once you have your goals and your plans, you need to begin. It has been said that it takes twenty-one days of repetition to form a habit. Therefore, determine that for the next twenty-one consecutive days you are going to take time to be alone with God, in His Word, prayerfully listening to the thoughts He will put into your heart and mind. As you spend this time, tell God you want only His thoughts and ask Him to make you aware of anything that is not truly from Him. Test everything by seeing if it is in agreement with the whole counsel of the Word of God.

And, *fifth,* begin examining every aspect of your life in the light of His coming. According to 1 John 3:2-3, our anticipation of the coming of the Lord acts as a purifying hope in our lives. Therefore, the days ahead should become days of cleansing as we put away those things—sins, habits, weights, possessions, activities, excesses—that keep us from pursuing His holiness (Hebrews 12:1-2,14).

Suppose our time is shorter than we think....

Someday—and it could be tomorrow or next year—the suppositions will be over. Jesus will appear. Then our opportunity to live the life of faith will be over.

Someday will come like a thief in the night. Don't be caught unaware.

Be ready...begin now. The discipline will pay eternal dividends.

"My beloved brethren, be steadfast, immovable, always abounding in the work of the Lord, knowing that your toil is not in vain in the Lord" (1 Corinthians 15:58).

My Response to His Words...

When You're Wondering If God Is Enough

How are you doing...really doing?

I would love to knock on your front door and have you invite me in for a cup of coffee and a chat. But since time and distance keep us from doing that, this book must be the next best thing. If we could just spend some time together, when we got past the "Hi! How are you?" I would want to know, "How are you doing...really doing?"

How are you doing on the inside? Are you hurting or feeling like a failure? Are you exhausted, tired of what seems like a rat race through the same old maze of life, day in and day out? Are you fighting a battle with disappointment?...depression?...discouragement? Are you feeling unloved or unlovable?

Are you questioning God, wondering why He has allowed things to be the way they are? Maybe you can't even admit this to others for fear they won't understand. Is there anger in your heart because of excruciating pain or bitter disappointment? Because you have lost someone or because your life has not been a "normal" life? Because you have been rejected, abused, neglected, or unloved?

Does the future scare you? Are you wondering about your job? Your health? Cancer? Heart problems? Your children? Are you wondering how you are going to care for your parents? How you are going to provide for your family? What will happen in your old age?

Are you worrying? Anxious because you may lose your job...or because you can't find work? Worried about the kids? About how they will turn out? About what they are being exposed to? What they might get into? Drugs? Immorality? Suicide?

Or, maybe all is well but you want to go deeper with God. You want a greater consistency of devotion to your Lord Jesus Christ. You want your life to be different, less commercial, more centered on your Lord and eternal things. You want your life to have eternal significance; you want to be used by Him more than you have been in the past.

Whatever your situation, wherever you are, the answer is always the same: *God knows your plight, your state. He knows exactly where you are and what you are going through.*

He knows, and He wants to give you a future and a hope. Because of this, His solution is always an eternal one, an all-sufficient one. And if you miss what I am saying, or if you pass it off, you are going to miss the answer to the void, hurt, disappointment, fear, or desire I have mentioned above. The answer is found in a verse of Scripture:

> *"A child will be born to us, a son will be given to us; and the government will rest on His shoulders; and His name will be called Wonderful Counselor, Mighty God, Eternal Father, Prince of Peace" (Isaiah 9:6).*

God has given you Jesus, His very own Son; and in giving you Jesus, He has put the government of your life on His shoulders.

No matter what your situation, feelings, or desires, you have Jesus as your *Wonderful Counselor.* Where are you running for help? Don't run anywhere unless your Wonderful Counselor tells you to, and then check out all you hear with Him. He is there to guide you, sustain you, care for you.

He is there to govern your life, and He can because He is the *Mighty God*—sovereign, in control of all, not permitting any accidents in your life. He is filtering every aspect of your life and the things that concern you through His omnipotent fingers of love. All that comes into your life will eventually work together for your good and His glory. It will be used to make you like Him, and if you will but cling to this in faith, on the day in which you see Him face-to-face, you will have no regrets (Romans 8:28-39).

Just remember, you have an *Eternal Father,* and you can snuggle in His all-sufficient arms. He is the Father who is always there, always ready to listen, always able to help, always wanting your best and seeing that you get it. He is never too busy, never plays favorites with His other children, and is always impartial. If you want to be mightily used by Him in His kingdom, He will see that it happens...as long as you listen to Him, obey Him, and serve Him without a divided heart.

The problem is, we have looked elsewhere for our help and consolation; we have not allowed Him to be our all in all. We have taken the government of our lives off His shoulders and we have turned to the arm of flesh.

Are you anxious, troubled, tormented? He is your *Prince of Peace.* Let not your heart be troubled, believe in Him, trust in Him. Peace will reign as long as you obediently cast all of your care upon Him (1 Peter 5:7). Stop being anxious for even one thing, but in everything—with prayer and supplication—make your requests known to Him. When you do, His peace will guard your heart and mind (Philippians 4:6-7).

So as we end our little chat, let me just remind you to place your trust upon His shoulders and turn your life over to your Wonderful Counselor, Mighty God, Eternal Father, and Prince of Peace who has the answer to every question, the solution to every problem, the wisdom for every decision.

"I will put my trust in Him" (Hebrews 2:13).

My Response to His Words...

When God Is Silent

Has there ever been a time when God seemed silent for so long that you questioned your relationship with Him?

Silent for so long that you even wonder if you imagined that you heard His voice? When you wonder if you ever really knew His wisdom and direction?

Have you ever experienced times when God seems so distant, so far away that the joy of His presence seems lost to you? A shroud covers your soul. You feel devoid of the emotions that once inflamed your soul in passion for your Lord and your God.

Heaven is silent. Winter has set in. Your heart shivers. The warmth of intimacy is gone. You try to rekindle a fire, but to no avail. Your spirit reaches out in the cold darkness to touch Him, only to confront lonely, numbing, confusing, discouraging...silence.

I must admit, there have been times in my life when God has been silent. When the joy and the sense of the deep intimacy of His presence have eluded me. When I felt I was hearing nothing new from His Word.

And it was hard, especially when others would share how He had been speaking to them. Sometimes it brought pain, sometimes doubt, and sometimes jealousy. Why was God speaking to them and not to me? What was I doing or not doing—or what should I have been doing in order to get God to reveal Himself to me as He was revealing Himself to others? Sometimes I even allowed pride to overtake me as I pretended to be able to relate to their joy.

But it's at times like that when I have been the most thankful for the years I have spent in the Word of God. For it is during the periods of silence—when our relationship with God seems devoid of joy and excitement and we don't know why—that we have to walk in the gut-level knowledge of all that we have studied. We have to believe God is there, that He has not moved, and that for some reason or other He has chosen to be "silent" for awhile.

God's silence is not like our human silence. When He is silent, it does not mean that He is not working or that He has abandoned us, the work of His hands. Oh, no!

God does not change, nor are His promises made null and void, for even "if we are faithless, He remains faithful, for He cannot deny Himself" (2 Timothy 2:13).

There is always a reason for God's silence—a purpose under heaven.

He may be silent because He has spoken and we have not responded—so He waits. Or He may have spoken and we have said "no"—so He gives us time to see the consequences of our disobedience. Or He may want to speak, but we are so busy that we are not giving Him the silence needed to hear His "still small voice" in the recesses of our hearts. Or God may be silent because it is *His* time to be silent.

In any intimate relationship there are always periods of silence. God's silence may be a test of our faith. Will we who fear the Lord, who obey the voice of His servant, who walk in darkness and have no light, trust in His name and rely on Him regardless of His silence (Isaiah 50:10)?

For it is then that we must wrap ourselves in His blanket of faith and our confidence in His Word; we must steep ourselves in His Word and cling to His promises. Cling, until He breaks the silence.

What God is doing is not without purpose, and when He does break the silence, our relationship with Him will be more treasured than before.

Madame Guyon, a French woman who lived during the reign of Louis XIV, knew a great deal about the silence of God. For seven years she was bereft of religious joy, peace, or emotions of any kind—a time of "privation or desolation."

> *During all that period, she had to walk by faith alone. She continued her devotions and her works of charity but without the pleasure and satisfaction she had previously felt....For seven years she kept looking for feelings and emotions before she learned to live above feelings and by simple faith in God. Then she found the life of faith is much lighter, holier, and happier than the life governed by feelings and emotions.*
>
> *Almost seven years after she lost her joy and emotion, [Madame Guyon] began to correspond with Father La Combe, whom she had been the means of leading into the light of salvation through faith some years previously. He was now the instrument of leading her out into the clear light and sunshine of Christian experience. He showed her that God had not forsaken her as she was so often tempted to believe but that He was crucifying the self-life in her.*
>
> *"I had a deep peace which seemed to pervade the whole soul, and resulted from the fact that all my desires were fulfilled in God. I feared nothing; that is, considered in its ultimate result and relations, because my strong faith placed God at the head of all perplexities and events. I desired nothing but what I now had, because I had full belief that, in my present state of mind, the results of each moment constituted the fulfillment of the Divine purposes. As a sanctified heart is always in harmony with the Divine providences, I had no will but the Divine will, of which such providences are the true and appropriate expression."*

What Madame Guyon learned, in essence, was that God was her all in all. He was all that mattered—not her emotions, not her desires, not her pleasures...only God. It was when she understood this that she began to walk in the totality of meekness.

Meekness is not weakness...it is strength. *His* strength. Meekness is accepting everything as coming from God without murmuring, disputing, or retaliating...even His silence.

Madame Guyon consecrated herself wholly to God; He could do with her as He pleased. She would no longer look to external experiences or internal joys. Instead she would find rest in His sovereign dealings, whatever they were.

Feel it or not, see it or not, hear it or not, she knew that "He Himself has said, 'I will never desert you, nor will I ever forsake you,' so that we confidently say, 'The LORD is my helper, I will not be afraid. What will man do to me?'" (Hebrews 13:5-6).

Her soul caught fire with this new depth of understanding, and as her soul caught fire, she lighted the way for the spirit of revival in almost every place she visited, and God used her mightily in France and many parts of Europe—until Louis XIV imprisoned her. But so great was her faith that her prison seemed a palace. She knew she was not forsaken; the Lord Jesus Christ was there—permitting the prison but sharing her cell.

Sometimes I know you, too, must feel forsaken, but you are not. He will not forsake you...He cannot forsake you. It would go against His very Word and character.

Why? Because God will never abandon the work of His hands. "He who began a good work in you will perfect it until the day of Christ Jesus" (Philippians 1:6).

Salvation is of the Lord. He is the One who chose you in Christ Jesus before the foundation of the world that you should be holy and blameless before Him (Ephesians 1:4). Therefore, what God began, God will complete. He "is able to keep you from stumbling, and to make you stand in the presence of His glory blameless with great joy" (Jude 24).

God may be silent—trials, testings, and challenges to our faith may come—but you and I can know with absolute surety that although we may be wounded, we cannot be defeated. God is watching over us. Whether we feel His presence and watchcare or not, God is there—maybe not manifesting Himself now but never ceasing to love us with His everlasting love and never failing to cause all things...even His silence...to work together for our good.

Once the seven years of silence were broken in the life of Madame Guyon, she was never the same. God's hand was upon her in an even mightier way. Her faith had been tested and proven: for although God seemed distant during that time, Madame Guyon did not veer from her profession of faith. She continued to walk in what she knew, learning to rely on what God had already spoken, rather than on how she felt.

It was in the very learning of this that she was enabled to live as more than a conqueror in the years to come when a king, empowered by Satan, would seek to destroy her faith by shutting her up in prison on two different occasions and then finally banishing her. Yet she spent the remainder of her life undefeated.

Even when He is silent, God's purpose is always victory, not defeat. So we can trust Him even in the silence.

Sometimes, however, we equate silence with separation, but with God that can never be true. God will never separate Himself from one of His children (Romans 8).

At times the Lord may seem distant, far away, unreachable, and uncommunicative in an intimate way. But you can know this: He is there. You and God are never apart. Separation from His love, from His promises, from Himself is impossible as far as God is concerned.

Silence?

It's possible.

Separation?

Absolutely impossible.

Like Madame Guyon and millions of others, we must continue to cling to the truths of His Word—even when He is silent. This is the assurance of faith, that nothing can separate us from our heavenly Father.

The apostle Paul poses the questions of a troubled heart in Romans 8:35:

> *"Who will separate us from the love of Christ? Will tribulation, or distress, or persecution, or famine, or nakedness, or peril, or sword?"*

And the answer, of course, is, "Nothing, and no one!"

The question I want to ask, however, is, "Why do we even have to ask?" We have to ask because of our own misconceptions.

Any time God is silent, or any time He allows His own to undergo difficult circumstances or situations, there is a tendency to think God has forsaken us. Otherwise, we would not be going through what we are going through!

We forget that in this life we are expendable for the sake of the furtherance of the gospel of the Lord Jesus Christ. As Paul wrote in Philippians 2:17:

> *"Even if I am being poured out as a drink offering upon the sacrifice and service of your faith, I rejoice and share my joy with you all."*

We human beings don't handle rejection very well. And when it comes to persecution and trials—well, our natural tendency is to wonder what we have done wrong to bring us into such painful difficulty. We have to be reminded that we are "considered as sheep to be slaughtered" for His sake and that death is to work in us so that life can work in others (Romans 8:36; 2 Corinthians 4:12).

Still, "in all these things we overwhelmingly conquer through Him who loved us." We conquer—not because of what we feel or because of what we experience—but because of who God is and where He is!

> *"Christ in you, the hope of glory"* *(Colossians 1:27).*

Nothing can separate us from the love of God.

If you are in, or ever enter, a period of silence in your relationship with the Lord, or if you ever enter into great trials of faith, it is crucial that you remember the declaration of faith penned by the apostle Paul and uttered by every succeeding generation:

> *"I am convinced that neither death, nor life, nor angels, nor principalities, nor things present, nor things to come, nor powers, nor height, nor depth, nor any other created thing, will be able to separate us from the love of God, which is in Christ Jesus our Lord"* *(Romans 8:38-39).*

These were not pious, lofty, poetic words needed to strike the match of faith. No, they were certainties of faith pounded out like steel in white-hot heat on the anvils of trials. This is the same man who wrote to the Corinthians, telling of beatings, stonings, dangers, robberies, sleepless nights, times of extreme hunger and thirst, imprisonment, exposure, and shipwreck that left him for a day and night in the deep (2 Corinthians 11:23-27). This is the man who testified that nothing could separate him from the love of God!

But, you may say, "That was the apostle Paul!" All right, then, let me show you the same proclamation from the lips of Madame Guyon. This frail but mighty woman of God lost everything this world affords. After ten years in a damp, dark, underground dungeon, she could write:

> *A little bird I am,*
> *Shut from the fields of air;*
> *And in my cage I sit and sing*
> *To Him who placed me there;*
> *Well pleased a prisoner to be,*
> *Because, my God, it pleases Thee.*
>
> *Naught have I else to do;*
> *I sing the whole day long;*
> *And He whom most I love to please*
> *Doth listen to my song;*
> *He caught and bound my wandering wing,*
> *But still He bends to hear me sing.*
>
> *My cage confines me round;*
> *Abroad I cannot fly;*
> *But though my wing is closely bound,*
> *My heart's at liberty.*
> *My prison walls cannot control*
> *The flight, the freedom, of my soul.*
>
> *O, it is good to soar*
> *These bolts and bars above,*
> *To Him whose purpose I adore,*
> *Whose providence I love;*
> *And in Thy mighty will to find*
> *The joy, the freedom, of the mind.*

Wouldn't you say that Paul and Madame Guyon—and many more like them through the centuries—have been more than conquerors through Him who loved them? For whether God was silent or not, they knew He still loved them; He had not forsaken them. And, Beloved, whether God is silent or not, He still loves you; He has not forsaken you. So what is to prevent you from living as more than a conqueror?

Even when God seems distant,
  even when He is silent,
    continue to walk by faith,
      trusting in His name.

Relying on all that He has said to us in His Word, then, we know that even in the silence He is working. And when eventually that silence is broken, the sound of His voice, the awareness of His presence will be glorious.

This is graphically illustrated in the history of Israel. Four hundred years of silence. That's what Israel endured during the intertestamental period, from the ringing words of the last prophet until the birth of Christ in Bethlehem. Four hundred years of silence. And yet God was there all the time.

The last words Israel heard as a nation were those spoken by Malachi the prophet. The silence was not broken until four hundred years later with the cry of John the Baptist in the wilderness: "Behold, the Lamb of God who takes away the sin of the world!" (John 1:29).

Glorious? I guess! Finally, Messiah had come! Messiah, the One promised to Adam and Eve when they sinned in Eden (Genesis 3:15)...the promise they had awaited for 4,000 years.

When I picture this in my mind, I see the Jews flocking out into the wilderness to hear the words of John the Baptist. Can you imagine their excitement? Four hundred years of silence broken.

And as I picture this, as I share their excitement, their awe, I cannot help but turn my thoughts to that moment when once again God will personally invade history and once again the world will hear His voice, for...

> *"the Lord Himself will descend from heaven with a shout, with the voice of the archangel and with the*

trumpet of God, and the dead in Christ will rise first.
Then we who are alive and remain will be caught up
together with them in the clouds to meet the Lord in
the air, and so we shall always be with the Lord"
(1 Thessalonians 4:16-17).

What a day, what a glorious day that will be! Never again will there be silence, never again a feeling of distance between you and your Lord. Never again shall a doubt of His love violate our faith; for we shall see God as He is, and we shall be with Him forevermore. Hallelujah!

We shall dwell in sweet union and communion forever and ever, and the sufferings of this present time will not be worthy to be compared with the glory that will be ours (Romans 8:18).

The final silence will be broken, and we will see Him as He is...as He has been...there all the time.

"My soul waits in silence for God only;
From Him is my salvation.
He only is my rock and my salvation,
My stronghold; I shall not be greatly shaken"
(Psalm 62:1-2).

MY RESPONSE TO HIS WORDS...

My Response to His Words...

When Pressures Build Up

Are you living life in overdrive? Do you ever feel like running away, checking out, giving up?

Life is filled with pressure, pressure, pressure.
Pressure to be.
Pressure to do.
Pressure to perform.
Pressure to produce.
And with the pressures come anxiety and stress, especially to the Christian who longs to be pleasing to God.

Am I being the mate I should be? The parent I should be? Am I handling everything the way I ought to as His child?

Life is so accelerated. Hurrying to work. Dashing to get the kids to their activities. Hurrying to prepare meals. Rushing to get to church.

You think you're going to slow down when the kids get back to school...come winter...come Christmas...come summer...come vacation.

But it doesn't happen. Or if you do slow down, it's not for long. Pretty soon you're back again in overdrive.

Realistically, life is never going to slow down; the pressure is never going to lessen; the stress will always be there in one form or another. So what are you going to do about it? Tough it out until you break? Run into some ungodly escape hatch? Give up? Check out?

The good news is: You don't have to choose any of the above. God knows about the pressure, the stress, the anxiety, the accelerated pace of our earthly life, and He has provided a "way of escape...so that you will be able to endure it" (1 Corinthians 10:13).

It's all wrapped up in our communion with God, what I call "going into the sanctuary." And there is one element of communion with God that I believe is a vital key to releasing pressure or stress. That key is worship through music: praising God in song. Let me share some Scriptures that show this to be true.

During Paul's second missionary journey, the apostle and his compatriot Silas found their ministry causing a riot, and they felt the brunt of it. Their clothes were torn from them, and they were beaten and thrown into prison.

Stress? Yes!

Anxiety? Every legitimate reason for it!

How did Paul and Silas handle it? What kept them from breaking?

Acts 16:25 gives us the answer: "But about midnight Paul and Silas were praying and singing hymns of praise to God." They turned their focus from the present pressures of their lives to the throne of their sovereign Abba Father—and the tension was relieved.

When sheep become tense, edgy, and restless, the shepherd will quietly move through the flock, and his very presence will release the tension of the sheep and quiet their anxieties. Their shepherd is there!

And this is what happens when we begin to worship our Lord and our God in song. We move into a consciousness of His presence, and the tension begins to unravel, the tautness of the pressure eases, anxieties become meaningless, for we are reminded that He is there—our Jehovah Shammah, our all-sufficient, sovereign God. He inhabits the praises of His people (Psalm 22:3).

Songs that stir your soul to worship, songs that bring tears of gratitude to your eyes, songs that cause a throbbing of holy passion for Christlikeness to swell within your breast. Songs that make you want to fall on your face or leap to your feet also have a physical effect upon your body, bringing sanctified release to physical tension.

Singing spiritual songs and making melody in your heart is God's way of delivering you from the stresses of the world.

> *"You are my hiding place; You preserve me from trouble; You surround me with songs of deliverance"* *(Psalm 32:7).*

Praising the Lord in song during my time alone with Him has drawn me into a depth of worship that I have never experienced before. The words of the music are engraved upon the tables of my heart and become an ever-present song upon my lips.

Try it. Make it a practice to worship God in song every day. Try beginning your day in song. Put your tape recorder in your bathroom or bedroom and play a worship tape while you're bathing and dressing. Sing in the shower. Carry tapes in your car to use as background music for singing His praises. Play music while you do housework. But, above all, make time daily to be alone and do nothing else but worship God in song.

The more you enter into His courts with praise and into His gates with thanksgiving, the less you will feel the stress, the pressure, the anxiety of daily life, for you will have...

> *"set your mind on the things above, not on the things that are on earth. For you have died and your life is hidden with Christ in God"* *(Colossians 3:2-3).*

MY RESPONSE TO HIS WORDS...

My Response to His Words...

When Life Is Bitter

How will you survive, when at times your very survival is being challenged?

Do you ever wonder how you are going to make it? Are you ever overwhelmed with the futility of going on? Are you ever weary in well doing? Are you ever tempted to envy the world? To look at the temporal instead of the eternal?

Are your trials and testings more than you can bear? Do you ever wonder, "Where is God in all this?"

Are you ever disappointed in your relationships with others? Do you ever feel alone...rejected...or trapped?

In any of these circumstances, what keeps you from slipping? From giving up? From walking out? From blowing it? How will you survive when at times your very survival is being challenged?

The secret is found "in the sanctuary," a term I use because it is a metaphor used in the Old Testament for communing with God.

When God told Moses to build the Tabernacle, He gave him a blueprint patterned after things in heaven (Hebrews 8:1-5). The Tabernacle was to be a sanctuary where God would dwell among His people (Exodus 25:8). God wanted His people to see that all of life was to be centered around communion with Him.

Why? Because we need His perspective on life. And when we don't have it...when we walk in our own ways...we always end up in frustration, emptiness, confusion, distortion, despair, desperation, destruction, or death.

As I listen to others, as I share their lives, and as I review my own life, I am more and more convinced that the answers to our problems are not found in "five easy steps" or "four principles of this or that" or in positive confessions and positive beliefs (note that I said positive, not proper!), but in intimate, knowledgeable relationship with our Father God and our Lord and Savior Jesus Christ, who sits at the right hand of the throne of God.

He bids us draw near with confidence to the throne of grace that we may receive mercy and find grace to help in time of need, that we may have access to all that is ours in His sanctuary.

In the sanctuary we gain a proper perspective of life and God becomes our all in all. In Psalm 73, the psalmist tells how envious and discouraged he was when he looked at the apparent prosperity and ease of the wicked. Bitterness crept into his life until he went into the sanctuary of God.

> *"When my heart was embittered and I was pierced within, then I was senseless and ignorant; I was like a beast before You. Nevertheless I am continually with You. You have taken hold of my right hand. With Your counsel You will guide me, and afterward receive me to glory. Whom have I in heaven but You? And besides You, I desire nothing on earth. My flesh and my heart may fail, but God is the strength of my heart and my portion forever"* (Psalm 73:21-26).

You'll never really be able to handle the bitterness and disappointments of life until God becomes your all in all. Until you get alone with your God consistently. If you don't, the things of this life will always be out of perspective!

In the sanctuary we learn God's ways. The seeming inequities of life, the ease of the wicked and the problems of the righteous, troubled the psalmist when he tried to understand them, "until I came into the sanctuary of God; then I perceived their end."

We forget that there is an end to this life as we know it and that what follows that "end" is judgment...everlasting, unending judgment for those who turn their back on God. "For, behold, those who are far from You will perish; You have destroyed all those who are unfaithful to You" (Psalm 73:27).

Oh, how we need to see that "thy way, O God, is in the sanctuary" (Psalm 77:13 KJV).

In the sanctuary we receive strength to go on. Have you ever thought, "It would just be easier to die"? The pressures of ministry were so great that it entered my mind one day. But because I live in the Word, I knew that the thought was not from God; it was Satan's subtle seduction, his tactics as a murderer (John 8:44).

In the sanctuary of His presence I received strength to go on...strength to resist, to persist, and to continue to be productive as a servant of the Most High God, El Elyon!

What about you? Do you need strength?

Remember, "Strength and beauty are in His sanctuary" (Psalm 96:6).

In the sanctuary we discover beauty: the beauty of His presence, the beauty of His person, the beauty of His purpose for our life. In the midst of all the ugliness of this world, of lives disfigured and distorted because of sin, we need beauty.

There's a beauty that comes from getting alone with God. Lines of stress, wrinkles of frustration, creases of bitterness are lifted from your face as you quietly, unhurriedly sit before your God...reading His Word, stopping to pray as He speaks to your heart, sorting things out, confessing, unloading all of your burdens, and listening. There, in His sanctuary, you gain assurance of His unlimited sovereignty and unconditional love, and it imparts a beauty to life...and to you.

Then you can walk out to meet your day, knowing that whatever happens you can make it, because you can say with the psalmist,

> *"As for me, the nearness of God is my good; I have made the Lord GOD my refuge"* (Psalm 73:28).

MY RESPONSE TO HIS WORDS...

My Response to His Words...

When Your Failures
Haunt You

Have you ever blown it?

Made a mistake...failed...sinned...and reaped the consequences?

You failed to consider the future...and now the future is here and it seems unbearable!

Or perhaps you know someone who is in this state and you hurt for them, but you don't know what to do...what to say...how to help.

> *"She did not consider her future.*
> *Therefore she has fallen astonishingly....*
> *'Is it nothing to all you who pass this way?*
> *Look and see if there is any pain like my pain*
> *Which was severely dealt out to me,*
> *Which the LORD inflicted on the day of His fierce*
>   *anger....*
> *For these things I weep;*
> *My eyes run down with water;*
> *Because far from me is a comforter,*

One who restores my soul....'
The joy of our hearts has ceased;
Our dancing has been turned into mourning.
The crown has fallen from our head;
Woe to us, for we have sinned!
Because of this our heart is faint;
Because of these things our eyes are dim"
(Lamentations 1:9,12,16; 5:15-17).

Many can identify with these words from Lamentations—maybe even you, Beloved. So much so, perhaps, that it is hard when I refer to you as "Beloved" because you don't feel like there is anything "beloved" about you.

I understand. Sometimes I look back at certain things I have done in the past since I have been a Christian...failures in ministry, in dealing with people...a wrong choice...failure to do something I should have done for another—but didn't.

I hate to fail, don't you?

Once a dear friend's husband died. Since I heard of it weeks after the fact, I did not make a concentrated effort to reach her. My negligence hurt her greatly, and when I realized it, I wept over this failure. Every time I thought of it, I hurt.

I could go on and on—to times I have not dealt with people with the sensitivity of Christ, to times when I have opened my big mouth and said something dumb, something that did not bring glory to my patient Lord.

Can you relate?

What do we do with feelings like these? How do we mend a heart broken by failure?

Or, what if we have sinned horrendous sins? What if what we have done makes these illustrations look like "Sunday school stuff" in comparison?

Like the children of Judah who were taken into captivity because of their sin and their failure to walk with God, we need the message of Lamentations. It is so pertinent today.

You need to read the whole book; it's only five chapters long. In fact, if you'll use *The New Inductive Study Bible* and follow the instructions I give for studying Lamentations, you'll experience for yourself the grace which is there for you. You'll see a passage that has ministered to me so greatly, for it tells us how to handle the memories of our failures—our sins of commission and omission, for...

> "The LORD'S lovingkindnesses indeed never cease, for His compassions never fail. They are new every morning; great is Your faithfulness" (3:22-23).

> "'The LORD is my portion,' says my soul, 'therefore I have hope in Him'" (3:24).

> "If He causes grief, then He will have compassion according to His abundant lovingkindness. For He does not afflict willingly or grieve the sons of men...[to] crush under His feet" (3:32-34a).

Listen to the infallible Word of God. Study it—and believe it—even if you don't feel it. It's not feelings that bring healing; it's faith. Believe Him. Hang on to the promises of God—bring them up against your feelings—live according to His Word, and, eventually, you'll find you can handle the failure. Then the failure will become your teacher rather than your executioner.

Walking in faith, believing what God says in Lamentations provides a future and a hope. It will bring you to the balm of Gilead, the Word of God, where you will be healed, cleansed, fed, nurtured, equipped, matured...and hear His "well done" because you have taken Him at His Word. Faith always pleases Him.

> "Restore us to You, O LORD, that we may be restored; renew our days as of old" (Lamentations 5:21).

My Response to His Words...

When You Think You Can Tolerate Sin in Your Life

Do you know what an awesome thing it is to serve God...to bear His name?

God is a God of love...a God of mercy...and when we fail Him, we can know that His compassions are new every morning and His mercies fail not (Lamentations 3:22-23).

Yet, because God is also holy—just and righteous in all His ways—we must remember that His judgment begins within His own household, with His own children (1 Peter 4:17).

"Be sure your sin will find you out" God warned the children of Israel—more specifically, the sons of Reuben and Gad (Numbers 32:23). He was speaking not to the heathen, the unbelieving, but to His own people. Those who had promised to follow and obey Him.

If we tolerate sin in our lives, God warns, we can be sure our sin will find us out.

Christians are those who have shuddered at the awfulness of their sin because they have seen the holiness of their God. They have seen His justice in dealing with sin at Calvary. They are people who have repented of their sin and turned from it, because they have seen sin for what it is: willful rebellion against the rulership of God over their lives. And in turning from their sin, they have embraced God's only means of dealing with sin, which is the death and resurrection of His Son, the Lord Jesus Christ, on their behalf.

Because of this identification with Christ, God cannot overlook sin in our lives. Therefore, He, our holy Father, will see that our sin will find us out.

How the church of Jesus Christ needs to hear this—that we might fear our God! How we need to remember that our God is immutable. He changes not...

God is the same yesterday...

When Achan disobeyed God and selfishly gathered up some spoils of war after the fall of Jericho—which God had expressly forbidden the Israelites to do—Achan's sin found him out, and God withdrew His protection. As a result, the children of Israel were defeated at Ai. All because there was "sin in the camp." (See Joshua 6–7.)

God is the same today...

Jesus warned His disciples:

> *"Beware of the leaven of the Pharisees, which is hypocrisy. But there is nothing covered up that will not be revealed, and hidden that will not be known. Accordingly, whatever you have said in the dark will be heard in the light, and what you have whispered in the inner rooms will be proclaimed upon the housetops"* *(Luke 12:1-3).*

Hypocrisy means wearing a mask. It is pretending to be one thing when in reality you are another. The Pharisees were those who pretended to be righteous, but inwardly they were not.

In describing the Pharisees' hypocrisy in Matthew 23, Jesus said that they cleaned the outside of a cup and a dish, but left the inside dirty—full of "robbery and self-indulgence" (23:25). Outwardly they appeared righteous to others, but inwardly they were "full of hypocrisy and lawlessness" (23:28). And then He said, "How will you escape the sentence of hell?" (23:33).

Nothing is hidden from God. We cannot pretend to be righteous on the outside while inside we are filled with unrighteousness. We can be sure our sin will find us out. The justice of God, the righteousness of God—the very character of God—requires it.

> *"For you are a holy people to the LORD your God; the LORD your God has chosen you to be a people for His own possession" (Deuteronomy 7:6a).*

My Response to His Words...

When You're Tempted to Settle for the Temporal

What are you investing in?

Those things which build up, nurture, and edify? Or that which is going to snare you, entrap you, make you ashamed, and eventually destroy you? Our holy God both commands and warns: "You shall be holy, for I am holy" (1 Peter 1:16). And if God says we are to be holy, then holiness is possible!

"Holy" means to be set apart unto God. Another word for holy is "sanctified." Which means that because God has set us aside for Himself, our lives—all that we are and do—are to be set aside for Him. We are not our own. We are His. Even our very breath is given to us by Him.

Your body is not your own...you cannot do with it as you please and please God (1 Corinthians 6:19-20; Galatians 5:16-17).

If we sow to the flesh, we will reap corruption. Our sins will find us out (Numbers 32:23)! But if we sow to the Spirit, we will reap eternal dividends (Galatians 6:8).

How my heart is burdened by the awful harvest so many are reaping...the pain, the snare, the destruction they've fallen into—and the futility of it all! It is time for us to stop and take a good look at what we are doing with our lives, our time, our energies, our bodies. We must become vigilant and walk circumspectly!

Our tendency is to spend all our time worrying about how we look on the outside. But God tells us to watch over our heart [mind] with all diligence, for it is what comes from the heart that defiles us. As we think, so are we.

> "The things that proceed out of the mouth come from the heart, and those defile the man. For out of the heart come evil thoughts, murders, adulteries, fornications, thefts, false witness, slanders. These are the things which defile the man" (Matthew 15:18-20).

What we do on the outside is merely a reflection of who we are on the inside.

Take a good look at your days…at the way you spend the weeks that fly by…at the year that is suddenly over.

There are so many who name the name of Christ who do not have time for God—time to get to know Him…time to meet with Him daily, time to pray, time to get to know His Word, time to share His love with others. Their time is consumed, instead, by self—then it's gone, never to be redeemed, because it hasn't been spent on eternal values.

God commands us to redeem the time—to buy it back, to control it and not to let it control you—because the days are evil (Ephesians 5:16). God wants us to invest our time and energies in things that have eternal value and in people whom He created for Himself, not in that which is useless, temporal, self-centered, or destructive!

What are you doing with your money? Are you spending it on earthly treasure, or are you making eternal investments? Are you laying up treasures on earth or in heaven?

When I was speaking in Memphis a few years ago, a woman heard me say that we were praying for $3,000 so that we could translate our Precept Bible studies into Chinese. At that very time the woman had been looking at a $3,000 Oriental rug that the salesman had assured her would last "forever." Instead, she made an "eternal" investment. She gave the $3,000 to Precept…and those equipped Chinese believers became her Oriental rug!

We will be held accountable for all of our investments. And while the rewards or losses begin even now, "in the present age" (Mark 10:28-31), these will not be known fully until there is no more time to change the course of our life.

When death comes, what has been done is done. There is no second chance, for our Lord will come quickly, and He will "render to every man according to what he has done" (Revelation 22:12).

Examine your life. And no matter what it costs, forsake that which is not of God and invest your life in that which has eternal value.

Pray about your investments. Find out how God wants you to use your mind, your time, your money.

> *"Be careful how you walk, not as unwise men but as wise, making the most of your time, because the days are evil" (Ephesians 5:15-16).*

My Response to His Words...

When Things Go Wrong

Give thanks in everything, God says.
Sometimes that's hard to do, isn't it?

Like when you miss a plane.

I was on a speaking trip that required me to go from Philadelphia to Houston to Los Angeles. In leaving Philadelphia, however, I got caught in traffic and missed my plane. I arrived at the airport only five minutes late, but in these days of jammed-up traffic patterns and late arrivals and takeoffs, this was one plane that was on time! And God didn't hold the plane!

Busy and tired as I was, the prospect of hours of delay loomed like a giant wall of frustration. In these circumstances, it was hard to "give thanks." At the time it simply seemed that all that would come from missing my plane was exhaustion.

But all I could see were the present circumstances. My view was limited from where my two feet stood on planet Earth.

> *"In everything give thanks; for this is God's will for you in Christ Jesus" (1 Thessalonians 5:18).*

Although we may know this Scripture backward and forward, when we cannot see any earthly reason for what has happened, it's hard to believe we should give thanks.

Our perspective is limited to the present: the present time, the present situation, the present inconvenience, the present pain, the present trial.

This present perspective ties our tongues so that instead of using them to say, "Thank You, Lord, although I do not understand," they wag back and forth in murmuring.

And although we may confine our murmuring under our breath, still it fills the air with discontent. Our nerves become taut with stress. The whole atmosphere becomes charged with electricity that could explode at any time.

It's hard to give thanks. And yet, hard or not, I know that when I do not give thanks, I am walking in unbelief. And unbelief is sin!

When I missed that plane in Philadelphia, I didn't stew about it in such a way that I acted or spoke unbecomingly. But I must admit I was a little stressed. I wished that I had control of the whole situation. Then things would have been different, and I wouldn't have missed the plane.

However, I would have missed what God had in mind.

What did He have in mind? A precious flight attendant who was hurting, confused, disillusioned. A woman who had a form of godliness, but needed Jesus.

And what else did God do so that I wouldn't miss her? Well, I finally got my connecting flight, but that flight never even went to Houston. By that time, Hurricane Gilbert was headed there, too, so they routed us straight to Los Angeles.

For "some reason" I wasn't able to sleep—wasn't even sleepy. So in the middle of the night, when most of the other passengers were curled up, stretched out, or zonked out, I was witness to the most majestic and awesome light show I have ever seen. God lit up the distant sky, showing off the magnificence of His cloud formations in a series of lightning flashes on three different stages; the light would dart from one to the other, then return to the first and move again to stage two and then to stage three. This went on for almost twenty minutes.

I had moved to a vacant window seat to get a better view, and one of the flight attendants came to gaze at the spectacle with me, saying that she had never seen anything like it. All that I could say as I peered out the window was, "How magnificent! Oh, isn't this wonderful? O Father, it's so awesome! As the lightning comes from the east to the west so shall the coming of the Son of Man be." I didn't know it at the time, but the stewardess was listening. After I returned to my seat, she came to where I was sitting. Leaning on the armrest across the aisle, she said, "I've seen you on television." It almost sounded like an accusation. I wondered why.

To make a long story short, she moved me up to a row of empty seats in first class where we could talk privately. Then I knew why I had missed my plane, why I was headed to Los Angeles and not Houston, and why God had put on His light show—it was for her. All this had been arranged for one precious, confused, and lost lamb. Awesome, isn't it?

At the time when I was to give thanks and rest in His sovereignty rather than be stressed out by the circumstances, I didn't know why. Usually God doesn't let us know—at least not right away. And sometimes we don't ever know. But He asks us to walk in faith...to thank Him in faith.

Because our sovereign God is never out of control, because He rules *over all*—the small and the big things of life, the tragedies and the triumphs—and because He loves us with an everlasting love, we can give thanks in everything.

> " 'I know the plans that I have for you,' declares the LORD, 'plans for welfare and not for calamity to give you a future and a hope' " (Jeremiah 29:11).

These words were spoken first to Israel, but they are for all of God's children, for He is the One who causes *all* things to work together for good to conform us to the image of His Son. Therefore, in *all* things—in everything—we can "give thanks."

> "We know that God causes all things to work together for good to those who love God, to those who are called according to His purpose" (Romans 8:28).

My Response to His Words...

When Skeptics
Question Your God

Do you ever worry about how you are going to "defend God" against the attack of unbelievers?

Are you surrounded by skeptics? Are you overwhelmed and oppressed by their godless lifestyle? Does their brashness shock you? Do their questions intimidate you?

One of the hardest situations for a Christian to handle occurs when a skeptic points out man's inhumanity toward man and asks where God is.

"If God is God, so great, so almighty, so loving, where is He when people are torturing and killing others?" That's always the question. And before the skeptic will even consider the gospel, he wants an answer. Period. End of argument.

What do you do? How do you answer? Man's inhumanity to man *is* taking place all the time in every corner of the world. *Why doesn't* God intervene? Perhaps you yourself even wonder sometimes: *Where is God—and why doesn't He do something?*

The skeptic's problem is twofold: He sees evil triumph over good, and he doesn't see God intervening to stop it. If God is who the skeptic thinks God ought to be, then God wouldn't allow things to be the way they are. This is why he's a skeptic.

Skeptics don't understand that God allows such things even though He is sovereign and can intervene any time He wants. They also are blind to the certainty of God's just judgment. God will judge, and His judgment will be just.

Another thing skeptics don't understand—and you may not either, although you are not a skeptic—is that God is not ruled by love alone. God is also holy, and God acts in accordance with the sum total of all His attributes.

Skeptics also fail to understand that God does not think like man. God is other than man, different from man.

Man is governed by his emotions, his desires, his limited knowledge and understanding. Man can try to predict the future, but he doesn't know it with certainty. He's not in charge of today—let alone tomorrow! Man may do what he wants, but he cannot totally control others. Man is limited by his own reasoning powers and his exposure to truth. Man is finite.

God is infinite. He sees all, knows all, and is eternal. An individual's unbelief in God and His sovereignty does not change the fact that God is in control. He allows evil (Isaiah 45:7). He can intervene and many times He does, but only when it suits His eternal purpose (Proverbs 16:4).

If you are going to live in His peace, you need to embrace in faith the fact that "the LORD is in His holy temple" (Habakkuk 2:20). Embrace it and be silent before Him.

You don't need to argue. You don't need to defend God! Simply explain Him as the Word of God explains Him. Then it is the skeptic's responsibility to accept or reject the Word of God. The responsibility is his, not yours. It's between him and God. It's a matter of faith. Whom will he believe? His own reasoning? Man's arguments? God's Word?

Whether the skeptic believes or not, God is not going to move out of His temple. He remains God. The skeptic can come into His temple through the cross of Jesus Christ and, in submission, bow the knee and confess that Jesus Christ is God. Or he can wait until hell and earth give him up with the rest of the dead, and he stands before God's Great White Throne to be judged according to his deeds which are written (Revelation 20:12-15).

Then, before being cast into the lake of fire where the worm dies not and the fire is not quenched, he will bow the knee and confess that Jesus Christ is God to the glory of the Father.

He will be without excuse (Romans 1:20). He could have known the truth if he had embraced in faith the One who said, "I am the way, and the truth, and the life; no one comes to the Father but through Me" (John 14:6). He could have had the mind of Christ to understand these things (1 Corinthians 2:16), but instead he chose to remain in the darkness of his own reasoning—and in doing so, he chose death. How sad! How very, very sad.

If you're like me, your spirit must be troubled not only at the blindness of men and women today, but at all that is going on in our world. I want so badly to do something about all of the corruption. I long to air our program *How Can I Live?* on primetime television and open up God's Word under His anointing and let people know where we're headed as a nation if we don't repent. Oh, that someone could be heard who would at least put the holy fear of God into people so they would think twice before they blatantly, needlessly rush headlong into iniquity and eventual, inevitable destruction.

When I think of this, I think of the book of Habakkuk. What an incredible book—so timely.

The prophet Habakkuk was frustrated. He saw the deep sin within his nation: the violence, the iniquity, the destruction, the strife, the contention. The law was ignored. Justice was never upheld. The wicked surrounded the righteous.

What was Habakkuk's recourse?

What is our recourse today in just such a society?

God—and He is enough.

We must lay our questions, frustrations, anxieties, and impotence at the feet of God and wait for His answer. And then, after receiving it, we must live by faith.

God assured Habakkuk that the ungodly would not go unpunished forever. Judgment would come.

But that knowledge is not enough. There is one more thing we need to be assured of—and it is this knowledge that keeps me plodding in the place of my appointment. It's the truth seen in God's final reassuring word to Habakkuk.

> *"The LORD answered me and said,*
> *'Record the vision*
> *And inscribe it on tablets,*
> *That the one who reads it may run.*
> *For the vision is yet for the appointed time;*
> *It hastens toward the goal, and it will not fail.*
> *Though it tarries, wait for it;*
> *For it will certainly come, it will not delay.*
> *Behold, as for the proud one,*
> *His soul is not right within him;*
> *But the righteous will live by his faith'"* (Habakkuk
> 2:2-4).

The world may be worshiping idols, the Lord goes on to say; justice may be perverted; wickedness may surround us; strife, destruction, and violence may be the order of the day—but God is not like the idols who cannot speak. God is in His holy temple.

He has pronounced His "woe to him who...." Sin will be judged. His judgment will come; it will not fail.

Let all the earth hush. They have no rebuttal, no excuse, no justified complaint, nothing to say to God. The wisdom, the cleverness of man, has failed. Man's impotence is obvious; his judgment sure.

God is God—immutable, eternal. All is under His control. God has overruled. What He has planned for Israel and for the church will come to pass.

Keep silent, O world. And you, child of God, live by your faith. You can. Faith will hold, because it is faith in the everlasting Sovereign Ruler of all the universe, the Creator of heaven and earth, the One who sits on the throne. He is in His holy temple.

I do not know what your specific trial or frustration is. I do not know what troubles you. I do not know the anxieties of your battle. But God does. What you do not understand, what you feel unable to cope with can be overcome moment by moment if you will live by faith and walk in communion with Him. The Lord will soon come for the salvation of His people.

You needn't cry out, "Lord, where are You?"

He's in His holy temple!

Be silent. Hush. It is all right, beloved of God.

> *"Though the fig tree should not blossom*
> *And there be no fruit on the vines,*
> *Though the yield of the olive should fail*
> *And the fields produce no food,*
> *Though the flock should be cut off from the fold*
> *And there be no cattle in the stalls,*
> *Yet I will exult in the LORD,*
> *I will rejoice in the God of my salvation.*
> *The Lord GOD is my strength,*
> *And He has made my feet like hinds' feet,*
> *And makes me walk on my high places"* (Habakkuk
>   *3:17-19).*

When You Want
to Call It Quits

---

*Are you hanging on
by your fingernails?*

Too worn, too weary, too weak to cry out to God anymore?

Are you ready to give up, to stop praying, to stop believing, to walk away?

Are you ready to call it quits because, as you see it, there is no way for anything to change?

Do you think, "I can't bear any more. I can't deal with the incessant pain"?

If I didn't know what I know about God, I might tell you to call it quits and to get on with your life.

But because God is who He is, because our times are in His hands, and because He's the God of all flesh and absolutely nothing is too hard for Him, I have to tell you not to give up. Don't "get on with your life." Wait, wait, I say, on the Lord.

And how do you wait on the Lord? There are two things you must do.

First, learn to sit at His feet and know Him.

When Martha complained to Jesus that her sister, Mary, wasn't in the kitchen helping her, Jesus replied:

> *" 'Martha, Martha, you are worried and bothered about*
> *so many things; but only one thing is necessary, for*
> *Mary has chosen the good part, which shall not be*
> *taken away from her' " (Luke 10:41-42).*

Can't we all identify with Martha? We're always preoccupied with the present business of life. We're always in a hurry, even with God.

We don't take time to let go, to relax, to be still and know that *He is God* (Psalm 46:10).

To do so involves a choice. It means that some things will not get done, that some people may not understand. But didn't Jesus say that sitting at His feet and hearing His Word was *the one thing which was needful—the thing which could never be taken away from us* (Luke 10:42)?

In other words, because of what you learn from Him and of Him, you'll always have something to hang on to—and it won't be by your fingernails!

Second, tell God you want only what He wants—whatever that means.

While such a statement, such a release of your will, your way, may terrify you at this point, it won't if you make it a practice to do the "first" thing that I mentioned: sit at His feet and know Him.

If you will give God your reputation,
…if you will seek no agenda other than God's,
…if your goal will be the same as Paul's—that Christ be exalted in your body whether by life or by death,
…if for you to live will be Christ and to die, gain,
…if you are willing to do His will no matter the cost,
…then you will never find yourself caught in despair.

Rather, you will find yourself waiting patiently on the Lord for His direction. His life will be your life…and your life, *His!*

Then whatever He says to you, do it—with confidence and without hesitation.

> *"Be still, and know that I am God; I will be exalted*
> *among the heathen, I will be exalted in the earth. The*
> *LORD of hosts is with us; the God of Jacob is our*
> *refuge. Selah" (Psalm 46:10-11 KJV).*

MY RESPONSE TO HIS WORDS...

My Response to His Words...

When You're Looking for Evidence of Genuine Faith

What are the marks of true Christianity?

Look around you, listen, and you will see or hear of Christians who are leaving their wives, divorcing their husbands, turning their backs on truths they once professed.

A Christian psychiatrist in a major city was accused of molesting one of his patients, a young boy. Upon close investigation, pictures were discovered that showed him participating in sexual acts with a number of different boys. The community was stunned. The family was in total shock. This man was a pillar in his church and his community! Had it not been for the pictures, they probably never would have believed the accusations that had been made.

What happened? How could a person who professed to believe in Jesus Christ ever live such a lifestyle?

Have you heard of people who at one time had a zeal for God, were excited about the Word of God, just couldn't get enough of Christianity, and then they walked away from it? Are you ever confused when you see people who were brought up under the Word of God run away from it? And what about those who get caught up in the worries of this life or the deceitfulness of riches and all of a sudden don't have time for the things of God?

Can a person who is truly saved walk, as a habit of life, where Jesus would never walk? Can a person say that he or she doesn't believe the Bible anymore and still be saved?

Basically, according to the Word of God, there are *seven* ways that you can tell the professors—those who merely name the name of Christ—from the possessors—those who are truly indwelt by Him. True Christianity brings forth lasting fruit—the evidence of salvation. So it's time we did some fruit inspecting.

> *"You did not choose Me but I chose you, and appointed you that you would go and bear fruit, and that your fruit would remain..." (John 15:16).*

The first fruit that gives evidence of a genuine faith is a person's walk.

> *"If we say that we have fellowship with Him and yet walk in the darkness, we lie and do not practice the truth" (1 John 1:6).*

A real Christian walks in light, not in darkness. A real Christian walks the way Jesus walked. A real Christian orders his or her behavior accordingly.

> *"By this we know that we are in Him: the one who says he abides in Him ought himself to walk in the same manner as He walked" (1 John 2:5b-6).*

Jesus is the light of the world. He did not walk in darkness; therefore, neither can those who are His true followers. Jesus said:

> *"I have come as Light into the world, so that everyone who believes in Me will not remain in darkness" (John 12:46).*

The second evidence of genuine faith is an outgrowth of the first: A real Christian does not live in habitual sin.

Oh, yes, we do sin (1 John 2:1-2), but it is no longer the habit of our lives. True Christians walk in obedience to His commandments. This is not to say that they don't disobey from time to time, but it will not be the habit of their lives. To not obey His commandments is to be lawless, and "sin is lawlessness" (1 John 3:4b).

> *"You know that He appeared in order to take away sins; and in Him there is no sin. No one who abides in Him sins [present tense in the Greek; therefore, it implies continuous or habitual action]; no one who sins has seen Him or knows Him....The one who practices sin is of the devil; for the devil has sinned from the beginning. The Son of God appeared for this purpose, to destroy the works of the devil. No one who is born of God practices sin, because His seed abides in him; and he cannot sin, because he is born of God" (1 John 3:5-6,8-9).*

A third evidence of genuine faith is a continued perseverance in the faith.

Can a person be saved and then, at some point, turn around and walk away from what he or she professed as clearly set forth in the Word of God?

The Bible speaks clearly of antichrists—those who seek to usurp the place of Christ in the life of a believer and, in doing so, to lead them astray from the faith.

> *"Children, it is the last hour; and just as you heard that antichrist is coming, even now many antichrists have appeared; from this we know that it is the last hour" (1 John 2:18).*

And what about those who follow such teachings that are contrary to the Word of God?

John tells us they never were really true believers:

> *"They went out from us, but they were not really of us; for if they had been of us, they would have remained with us; but they went out, so that it would be shown that they all are not of us" (1 John 2:19).*

The fruit of true Christianity is perseverance in the faith. Mark it well, Beloved. True believers do not permanently stray from God.

Also, a true Christian cannot help but love others...

> *"because the love of God has been poured out within our hearts through the Holy Spirit who was given to us"* *(Romans 5:5).*

This is the fourth evidence of genuine faith—that we love one another.

> *"We know that we have passed out of death into life, because we love the brethren. He who does not love abides in death"* *(1 John 3:14).*

Because love is an attribute of God, and because a Christian is a person who is indwelt by God, then it is only logical that love would be a fruit that a child of God would bear!

John emphasizes this in his short epistle, making it clear that if there is no love for others, then you are not His!

Watch how he uses the word "know."

> *"Whoever believes that Jesus is the Christ is born of God, and whoever loves the Father loves the child born of Him. By this we know that we love the children of God, when we love God and observe His commandments"* *(1 John 5:1-2).*
>
> *"Everyone who hates his brother is a murderer; and you know that no murderer has eternal life abiding in him"* *(1 John 3:15).*

The fifth evidence of genuine faith is a life that overcomes the world.

A true Christian is not overcome by the world. Instead, because Christ is in us and because He, by the Holy Spirit, enables us to keep His commandments, we are able to overcome the world.

> *"This is the love of God, that we keep His commandments; and His commandments are not burdensome"* *(1 John 5:3).*

Note this—it is so essential. It is not a burden for a believer to walk in righteousness and to be obedient. We may fail now and then, but it should never be because it is a burden! If we fail, it is because we have chosen to walk by the flesh rather than by the Spirit,

> *"for whatever is born of God overcomes the world; and this is the victory that has overcome the world—our faith. Who is the one who overcomes the world, but he who believes that Jesus is the Son of God?"* (1 John 5:4-5).

"The whole world lies in the power of the evil one," but praise God that "greater is He who is in you than he who is in the world" (1 John 5:19b; 4:4b).

The sixth evidence of genuine faith is the inward witness of the Spirit of God testifying that He resides within.

> *"By this we know that we abide in Him and He in us, because He has given us of His Spirit"* (1 John 4:13).

And while this fruit may seem totally subjective, it is not. For if a person says that he has the witness of the Spirit in his heart, he will also have all the other evidences of salvation that we have already mentioned. These manifestations of genuine Christianity will be evident at one degree or another throughout the Christian's sojourn here on earth.

As you meditate on these truths, Beloved, what is God saying to your own heart? Or is He laying someone on your heart for prayer?

What is your relationship to the Word of God? How well do you understand it? What is life like without it? Could you live without it? Would it make any difference if the government took away your Bible?

Or let me put it another way: Have you ever wondered why people would risk their jobs, their freedom, their relationship with their loved ones, even their very lives for the Word of God? This happened for years behind the Iron Curtain and is still happening today in many countries around the world.

Why? Why is the Word more precious than freedom?

Because within the soul of every child of God there is a spiritual craving, a hunger and thirst for righteousness.

"Man does not live by bread alone, but man lives by everything that proceeds out of the mouth of the LORD"(Deuteronomy 8:3b).

In the Sermon on the Mount our Lord said:

"Blessed are those who hunger and thirst for righteousness, for they shall be satisfied" (Matthew 5:6).

Once the Holy Spirit moves in a person's heart—convicting of sin, righteousness, and judgment—there is an awakening of a thirst for righteousness, a longing to be finished with sin and its awful harvest. Then, when in salvation the Holy Spirit takes up His residence within a child of God, the Spirit causes him to set his mind on the things of the Spirit (Romans 8:1-8).

It is the Spirit of God within us that enables us to understand the things of God. This is one of the ways you know that you are truly born again. You have a hungering and thirsting for righteousness that drives you to the Word of God. And when you get there, you find that you can understand it! The veil comes off when Christ comes in! And it happens because of the indwelling Spirit.

"As it is written, Eye hath not seen, nor ear heard, neither have entered into the heart of man, the things which God hath prepared for them that love him. But God hath revealed them unto us by his Spirit: for the Spirit searcheth all things, yea, the deep things of God. For what man knoweth the things of a man, save the spirit of man which is in him? Even so the things of God knoweth no man, but the Spirit of God. Now we have received, not the spirit of the world, but the spirit which is of God; that we might know the things that are freely given to us of God" (1 Corinthians 2:9-12 KJV).

Have you ever wondered why, before you were saved, the Bible seemed boring and hard to understand, but after you were saved, you couldn't get enough? Finally you could understand it! And it was interesting and exciting!

Now you understand, don't you? Without God's Spirit inside us, we cannot understand the things of God! In fact, to the natural (unsaved) man or woman, the things of the Spirit of God are foolishness (1 Corinthians 2:14).

This is the seventh evidence of genuine faith. You can tell the saved from the lost because the saved are hungry for His Word and His righteousness.

Aren't you just awed at the mystery of salvation? One minute a person is lost, and the next minute he or she is saved!

You don't see anything spectacular or mysterious taking place; and yet, all of a sudden, the person is a brand-new creature in Christ Jesus, indwelt by the Spirit of God because he has been born again. And when he is, his life begins to evidence these seven "good fruits."

- A Christian walks in the light, following in the footsteps of Jesus.

- A Christian does not walk in darkness, living in habitual sin.

- A Christian does not permanently stray from God, but perseveres in the faith.

- A Christian loves other people.

- A Christian walks in righteousness, overcoming the world.

- A Christian has the witness of the Holy Spirit in his heart.

- A Christian hungers for His Word and His righteousness.

"These things I have written to you who believe in the name of the Son of God, so that you may know that you have eternal life" (1 John 5:13).

MY RESPONSE TO HIS WORDS...

My Response to His Words...

When You're Rejected or Laughed At

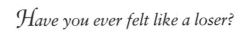

Have you ever felt like a loser?

Have you ever found yourself in a situation where you looked like a loser—and felt like one? It's hard, isn't it?

Christians can look like losers, too.

I remember a difficult situation my husband, Jack, and I faced several years ago. It was probably the hardest thing we have ever faced together.

Jack and I found ourselves in circumstances which made us and our Christianity look like real losers, real failures. We were in an environment so contrary to our Christian beliefs and way of life that it was like being in a foreign land and realizing you couldn't communicate with the people because you didn't speak the same language. It was a real culture shock, to say the least! This situation was hard enough, but it was nothing in comparison to the times that followed!

We looked like losers. We were denounced as losers. And those who were associated with us were to be most pitied.

I thought my heart would break...and then God took me to the cross.

As I read through and pored over the Gospels of Matthew, Mark, and Luke, my heavenly Father reminded me that He had called me to a cross—death to self, death to the opinions and affections of others, even those closest to me. Death to my dreams, my hopes, my desires—death to self.

Jesus Christ alone is to be my one desire—His life, not mine. I am to love Him above all else, above all others. And if choices are to be made, I must choose Him and His truth no matter what I lose, no matter how often I am thought "a loser."

Then my heavenly Father reminded me of what His own Son had experienced.

Suspended between heaven and hell, Jesus found no comfort nor comforter. His friends had forsaken Him. One had even betrayed Him. The Jews who had called for His crucifixion taunted Him. The criminals cursed Him. The sun refused its light.

Then His own Father forsook Him, as Jesus who knew no sin was made to be sin for you and me—and for those who think we are losers.

So much had been expected of Him. So much had been proclaimed about Him. And there He hung in the midst of common criminals—raw, beaten, bloody, gasping for breath, and crying out that He was thirsty, even though He had claimed to be the fountain of living waters.

Jesus didn't look like the King of kings that day. Jesus looked like the loser of losers!

But the end of the story hadn't been told…

And neither has the end of your story or mine!

I don't know what your pain is. I don't know what failure you deal with…what inadequacies you wrestle with…what shattered hopes or dreams plague you…what wrong judgments haunt you.

But I can tell you this: If you belong to the Lord Jesus Christ, you may look like a loser, you may be called a loser, you may be despised, rejected, laughed at, scorned, talked about, and deemed a loser, *but* you're not!

The final chapter hasn't been written yet!

While you are not perfect—any more than any other child of God is perfect—you belong to Jesus, and Jesus belongs to God!

You've been redeemed from the slave market of sin, bought by His precious blood. You have been made part of a kingdom of priests who will reign with Him when He comes as King of kings and Lord of lords.

As children of God, we're not losers. We're winners, simply by faith in our Lord Jesus Christ!

Now live in that "rest of faith." He who is coming will soon come.

> *"And they sang a new song, saying, 'Worthy are You to take the book and to break its seals; for You were slain, and purchased for God with Your blood men from every tribe and tongue and people and nation. You have made them to be a kingdom and priests to our God; and they will reign upon the earth'"* *(Revelation 5:9-10).*

MY RESPONSE TO HIS WORDS...

My Response to His Words...

Words of
OBEDIENCE

When You're Disappointed, Discouraged, Defeated...

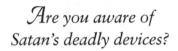

Are you aware of
Satan's deadly devices?

Has disappointment in a person or a situation ever caused you to go into an emotional tailspin?

Have you ever felt you might drown in your discouragement?

Have you ever fallen into a well of dejection and despaired to the point where you were so demoralized that you simply sat down and didn't attempt to climb out?

Then, my friend, you have engaged in warfare with the evil one, who desires to take you captive; and you have allowed him to penetrate your line of defense with his armored division and his foot soldiers.

You have done battle with Satan's Five Deadly D's and tasted their awful wretchedness.

The first deadly D is *Disappointment*. To counterattack disappointment you need to launch the Christian's Strategic Defense System (SDS) of faith that in meekness praises God in every situation by seeing it as God's sovereign appointment. Change the *D* of Disappointment to an *H*, and you have His Appointment.

If you refuse to do this, if you refuse to give thanks in everything, believing that this is the will of God in Christ Jesus concerning you, then the next deadly D the enemy will launch against you is *Discouragement.*

To become discouraged is to become disheartened—to be weakened, to lose your courage so that you think there is no way you can win. When this happens, you throw up your hands and say, "I'll never make it! I'll never survive. It's no use, I'll never get out of this one."

Unless you deal with discouragement—head it off at the pass—there is no way to be the victor.

After Moses died, God was careful to admonish his successor, Joshua, to "be strong and courageous" as he led the children of Israel into the long-awaited Promised Land. God repeats himself three times as He says to Joshua: "Be strong and courageous" (Joshua 1:6-9). Courage rather than discouragement would bring the children of Israel into the promises of God.

Years earlier, the children of Israel had lost the battle with discouragement at Kadesh-Barnea. Instead of being strong and facing their enemies in faith, the Israelites had believed the report of the ten spies, who had become discouraged by the sight of giants in the land. As a result, they had spent forty years wandering in the wilderness.

What about you? Have you listened to the world's analysis of your condition or your future rather than being strong and courageously believing your God?

If so, then you have found yourself mired in the mud of *Dejection.*

Instead of the joy of the Lord being your strength, as Nehemiah exhorts his people (Nehemiah 8:10), you are about to faint (Isaiah 61:3). When dejection pulls you down into its depths, you face lowness of spirit and emotional fatigue. The oil of gladness has been exchanged for mourning, and you have not covered yourself with a spirit of praise. Either you praise God in pure, gut-level faith, whether you feel it or not, or you will continue to weaken.

Then you will find yourself in *Despair,* having lost or abandoned hope. Despair leaves you apathetic; your mind is numb. And if this goes unchecked, you may find yourself acting recklessly, not considering the consequences of your actions. Desperation is energized despair, and in this state you do things which you later greatly regret, but which many times bring lifelong consequences.

Often you see examples of this when people suddenly find themselves confronted by the infidelity of their mate or the demand for a divorce, or when they are faced with financial reversal. During the Great Depression in America, many despairing businessmen opened the windows of their offices and jumped to their deaths. Others put a gun to their head and pulled the trigger! They reacted in the flesh and the rationale of their own minds, and the consequences were deadly.

When you find yourself in a state of despair, you need to say with the psalmist,

> *"Why are you in despair, O my soul? And why have you become disturbed within me? Hope in God, for I shall again praise Him for the help of His presence"* *(Psalm 42:5).*

When you are in despair, write down why and then look for a specific promise of God to write next to each cause of your despair. If you don't, you'll find yourself *Demoralized.* And demoralized people run in circles—if they even have the strength to run! They are cast into disorder. They cannot get their act together in their home or in their business affairs or in any of the disciplines of life. Many times they are simply paralyzed with fear.

But God has not given you "the spirit of fear; but of power, and of love, and of a sound mind" (2 Timothy 1:7 KJV). His is the power, the glory, and the victory; so when the Five Deadly D's are launched against you, you can be more than a conqueror of this enemy of your soul.

> *"Whatever is born of God overcomes the world; and this is the victory that has overcome the world—our faith"* *(1 John 5:4).*

My Response to His Words...

When You're Locked in a Prison of Difficult Circumstances

Have people, things, or circumstances robbed you of your joy?

Did you know that no matter what comes your way in the course of your life, you can have joy? Joy...no matter what! Does this sound like a pipe dream or some spiritual fantasy? Well, it's not. In fact, the book of Philippians assures us that "joy no matter what" can become a reality for those who would grasp this truth and live accordingly.

Paul wrote to the Philippians while he was a prisoner of Rome...imprisoned for preaching the gospel of Jesus Christ, and in his short but powerfully practical letter to them, Paul uses the word "joy" or "rejoice" sixteen times.

> *"Now I want you to know, brethren, that my circumstances have turned out for the greater progress of the gospel....Christ is proclaimed; and in this I rejoice. Yes, and I will rejoice" (Philippians 1:12,18).*

All prisons are not concrete cells with steel bars and iron doors. Some people are imprisoned in an unhappy marriage, living with a selfish, indifferent, or even cruel mate. Others find themselves locked into an unhappy, hard, difficult, or seemingly impossible situation. Or the captivity may be a physical one—imprisoned in a body that will not function as it ought. As a quadriplegic, my friend Joni Eareckson Tada lives in this type of prison...and yet because of her joy, her prison has become a platform for the gospel and the sufficiency of Christ. And the joy of the Lord has become her strength.

What if you found yourself in such a prison? Would the joy of the Lord become your strength? Would you have the key to unlock that prison and step out into the joy of the Lord?

The key to having joy no matter what is found in the person of Jesus Christ and in a mind-set or attitude that is submissive to His will. (Christ is mentioned thirty-six times in Philippians, not counting all the other nouns or pronouns that refer to Him, and "mind" or "attitude" is used ten times.)

In Philippians 1:21 Paul tells us that Christ is his very life. "For to me, to live is Christ and to die is gain," he said. Paul's joy was not centered in his freedom from prison, whatever form that imprisonment might take. Rather, his joy was wrapped up in the person of Christ. Christ was his life. Therefore, it did not matter whether he was locked up or free. For his life was consumed by one desire:

> *"According to my earnest expectation and hope,...I will not be put to shame in anything, but...with all boldness, Christ will even now, as always, be exalted in my body, whether by life or by death" (Philippians 1:20).*

Whatever God wanted to do with Paul was all right, for Paul's heart and mind was set on one thing: God's will for him. Paul knew God, not man, held the keys to his prison doors. God shuts and God opens. Paul's life was so consumed with the love of Christ that he actually preferred to die and be with his God (Philippians 1:22-26). However, Paul also knew that his imprisonment was "for the greater progress of the gospel" (1:12).

Oh, dear child of God, whatever you are enduring now—or whatever comes your way in the future—it is not without purpose in the sovereignty of God. If you will let Christ be your life and if you will have a submissive mind toward God, you will have joy. And your joy, in spite of imprisonment, will be used by God to reach others.

As I write this, God has brought one of our dear Precept trainers to mind—a young, attractive wife and mother who is also extremely gifted as a teacher. When this young woman discovered that she had multiple sclerosis, she wrote to me, saying,

> *God knew that if He chose for me to live in a wheelchair, I would seek to do so to His glory. Through it all, God is teaching me to live a much more disciplined life. He has given me another area in which I must live in total dependence upon Him, and in some ways I feel my walking through the situation will benefit others. As I prayed one day, I simply spoke 2 Corinthians 4:8-9: "I am hard pressed on every side, but not abandoned; struck down, but not destroyed." I told God that would be my "theme," but He said "no."*
>
> *The song of my heart was to be found further on down in that chapter in verses 15-18 (NIV): "All this is for your benefit, so that the grace that is reaching more and more people may cause thanksgiving to overflow to the glory of God. Therefore we do not lose heart. Though outwardly we are wasting away, yet inwardly we are being renewed day by day. For our light and momentary troubles are achieving for us an eternal glory that far outweighs them all. So we fix our eyes not on what is seen, but on what is unseen. For what is seen is temporary, but what is unseen is eternal."*

Truly, my precious friend and co-laborer has joy...joy no matter what.

Pray through Philippians 1, substituting your circumstances for Paul's. Make his desire yours. Practice having his mind-set, and claim the joy that will be yours. And know this: Your life shall then have a greater eternal impact. (Read the book of Philippians. Mark each use of "joy" or "rejoice," "Christ," "mind" or "attitude." Then write down what you learn from marking each word.)

> *"Finally, my brethren, rejoice in the Lord. To write the same things again is no trouble to me, and it is a safeguard for you"* (Philippians 3:1).

My Response to His Words...

When Joy Is Shattered

Have people ever
robbed you of your joy?

Perhaps someone spoke a cross or painful or critical word, and in an instant your joy was gone.

How did you respond?

Possibly the phone rang…a letter came…a friend stopped by…and what you learned shattered your joy! Maybe it was something about your child, your mate, your friend—and in that moment the sun ceased to shine. Darkness and gloom hovered over your heart.

What did you do?

Or did disappointment rob you of your joy? Disappointment because another's fortune was better than your own? Disappointment over another's failure to be to you what they should have been?

How did you react?

People can rob us of our joy in so many ways—unless we learn to have the mind of Christ.

We are living in a time of unprecedented selfishness, where the emphasis is on the individual's personal needs and happiness rather than the good of others and the welfare of the whole. Today the rallying cry is "Be number one." But when being number one is our goal, then everyone else must be in second place—including God.

Is this what happiness and joy are all about? Or, should I say, is this what Christianity is all about?

Not according to the Word of God or to the example set by our Lord Jesus Christ!

In Philippians 2:5-8 Paul exhorts us to have the mind of Christ. Listen to his words with hearing ears:

> *"Have this attitude in yourselves [or, "let this mind be in you"] which was also in Christ Jesus, who, although He existed in the form of God, did not regard equality with God a thing to be grasped, but emptied Himself, taking the form of a bond-servant, and being made in the likeness of men. Being found in appearance as a man, He humbled Himself by becoming obedient to the point of death, even death on a cross."*

The mind of Christ is a servant mind: a mind that puts obedience to God above everything else; a mind that puts others before self. It is a mind that does not insist on being "number one."

Take a few minutes to read Philippians 2…right now. See how, throughout this chapter, we find that this servant mind is modeled not only by our precious Lord, but also by those who bear His name.

Paul demonstrates this mind when he says:

> *"Even if I am being poured out as a drink offering upon the sacrifice and service of your faith, I rejoice and share my joy with you all" (Philippians 2:17).*

But Paul is not our only example in this chapter; there is also Timothy who served Paul as a son in the furtherance of the gospel. And there is Epaphroditus who, out of concern for others, "came close to death for the work of Christ" (see Philippians 2:25-30).

Could this be said of you? Are you concerned for the spiritual welfare of others? For the hurting world of people who need God's Word, as well as our love, care, and concern? Are you willing to give yourself to listening to them, to helping them, to meeting their needs, to showing them what God has to say in His Word? Are you willing to take time or make time to pray for them?

In other words, do you have the servant mind of Christ?

Oh, how we need to say, "Here am I, Lord. Use me. Send me."

I recall a time when I was in Singapore carrying out a very busy schedule of teaching and speaking engagements. On my one free evening, a young man from that city approached me and asked if he could meet with me for counseling. I must confess I was torn at first about adding time with him to an already busy schedule, but I told him I could give him 45 minutes. (Our time together lasted almost two-and-a-half hours!)

This young man told me that he had been involved in sin with another man for over two years and wanted to commit suicide. As I held him in my arms while he sobbed over the grievousness of his sin, I listened to his tender words of confession to the Lover of his soul, the One whom he was to love above all else.

Later, as we sat over coffee and I saw the joy that now radiated from his countenance, I thanked God that I had considered this man's concerns above my own schedule and my own pressures. The joy over his repentance was wonderful, but the joy that came because I had been obedient to God's command to have the mind of Christ was far greater.

Sometimes the joy of obedience does not bring such immediate results. It is then we must be reminded of the much greater burden our Lord bore in humbling Himself unto death, for during His trial and horrible scourging, His tormentors did not realize that this one they mocked as "the king of the Jews" was about to bear their sins so that they might have eternal life simply by repenting and believing on Him.

Although we may not see any results from our witnessing, there is still the sense of sweet inward joy because we know we've done what we should.

It is not people who should rob us of our joy; it is our failure to have the mind of Christ that should do so. Our lives are to be lived for the sake of others. We are to be obedient servants, like our Lord, who "came not to be ministered unto, but to minister, and to give his life a ransom for many" (see Mark 10:42-45 KJV).

Therefore, when you start to lose your joy because of people, stop and ask God how He would have you serve Him in this particular situation.

> *"Do nothing from selfishness or empty conceit, but with humility of mind regard one another as more important than yourselves; do not merely look out for your own personal interests, but also for the interests of others. Have this attitude in yourselves which was also in Christ Jesus" (Philippians 2:3-5).*

My Response to His Words...

When Your Joy
Is Clouded Over

*Have things ever robbed you of
your joy?*

Has something of temporal value ever become so important to
you that your joy in the Lord does a vanishing act? Your preoccu-
pation with that "thing" casts a cloud that obliterates the warmth
of a concentrated devotion to your Lord?

Maybe it is something tangible...or maybe it is some "thing" in
your past that you cannot seem to shake.

Can you say, "Yes, I can relate! I have been there"?

Well, Beloved, so have I.

I will never forget the time when bedsheets robbed me of my
joy!

Imagine! Losing your joy over something as simple and mundane
as bedsheets when there is a whole world out there in desperate need
of knowing our Lord and His Word. (And if you men think you
can't relate to this, just substitute something that has to do with your
car—like tires!)

Years ago when we first purchased what is now called the Precept Ministries Conference Center, we moved into an old yellow

farmhouse on the property. One of the first things we did to "make it home" was to redecorate our bedroom with some attractive dark blue wallpaper I found on a discount rack. I was excited! The room looked so handsome now. The bedspread, curtains, and rugs were all coordinated—everything except the sheets! But that was no problem. Our one and only set of king-sized sheets was due for a replacement. What wonderful timing!

So I went out to roam the discount stores and sale racks looking for coordinating sheets. Two sets caught my eye. One was perfect, but the matching pillowcases were sold out. Although pillowcases were available for the other set, that was my second choice because the color was a lighter shade of blue than the wallpaper. This was to be my only set of sheets, so I wanted them to look just right. I stood there debating and debating, and finally decided I'd take my chances and get the set without the pillowcases. I reasoned that, since it was a name brand, I'd be able to find the matching pillowcases elsewhere.

I rushed home, put my new treasures on the bed, and stood back and looked at the effect with great satisfaction. As I snuggled into sleep that night, I shut out any doubts about what I would do if I didn't find pillowcases to match the sheets I was now sleeping on.

The next morning I hit the stores again—and guess what? You're right. I couldn't find matching pillowcases anywhere. And we had already slept on our new sheets!

Suddenly, my joy was gone!

Would you believe that from that day on, "sheets" were all I could think of?

I would try to study, and I would think sheets.

I'd be teaching, and all of a sudden my mind would be covered over with those sheets.

I'd start my quiet time, and my eyes would drift over to the bed, and all I could think about was *sheets!*

And with every remembrance of sheets, I would beat myself mentally for not buying the light blue ones with matching pillow-cases.

A set of sheets had robbed me of my joy!

Isn't that ridiculous?

Yes. But I'm sure you have your own story of how some "thing" robbed you of your joy. Something as small as sheets...or as significant as your job!

How do you handle situations like this that can drive you up the wall and keep your focus off the things that really matter—like the joy of the Lord and our need for Christlikeness?

Well, let's look at Philippians 3 and see what we can learn and then live by when "things" start to rob us of our joy. Let's begin by reading several verses from this wonderful chapter and underlining every use of the word "things."

Paul writes:

> *"Whatever things were gain to me, those things I have counted as loss for the sake of Christ. More than that, I count all things to be loss in view of the surpassing value of knowing Christ Jesus my Lord, for whom I have suffered the loss of all things, and count them but rubbish so that I may gain Christ....Brethren, I do not regard myself as having laid hold of it yet; but one thing I do: forgetting what lies behind and reaching forward to what lies ahead, I press on toward the goal for the prize of the upward call of God in Christ Jesus" (Philippians 3:7-8,13-14).*

Paul's past associations and achievements had been important to him. If you will read Philippians 3:4-6 you will find that Paul wasn't into "pretty things," but he was into achievements of the flesh. We each have our own set of "things" that mean something to us, and when they are lost or disturbed, we can be robbed of our joy.

Paul knew this. Yet he also knew that only one thing could or should be central or important to him, and that thing was Christlikeness! So, he determined, he would develop a *single mind by making Christ his goal!*

To do this, Paul literally had to count all things as loss for the excellence of knowing Jesus Christ. In comparison to knowing Christ, everything else was rubbish.

Instead of focusing on things as they might have been or might be, Paul set his eyes on the goal. Forgetting the things that were past, he reached forward to what lay ahead—Jesus Christ.

And that's what I had to do, too. I got over my disappointment about the sheets by talking it over with my Lord and God. I told Him that I realized that sheets were temporal and that He was eternal.

When I stand before Him, one second in eternity will erase all care or thought of anything except whether or not I allowed the situations of life to make me more like Him. Christlikeness is all that will matter.

Therefore, I knew that I had to forget those things which were behind. I couldn't change them. All I could do was go forward, learning from my mistakes but not dwelling on them. A divided mind would keep my eyes off the goal. If I was going to run the race set before me, I could only look in one direction, and that was straight forward...pressing on.

And so I say to you, dear one: Let that thing—whatever it is—go. It will only hinder you from getting on with what God has for you. And when "things," even those that are cause for celebration or expectation, begin to rob you of your joy, try the following:

- Take a careful look at the "thing" in the light of eternity. What does it have to do with the eternal? If it has no value, release it.

- Ask yourself if the "thing" is worthy of the energy you are expending on it. Are you fretting over something you cannot change? Is it distracting you from the things of God? Then, in an act of discipline, put it out of your mind. Every time the thought of "it" returns, knocking at the door of your mind, begging refuge, refuse it.

- Can you change the "thing," turn it around, rectify it, live without it? If there is nothing you can do to change it, then be obedient, walk in faith, and forget those things which are behind and press on toward the prize of your high calling in Christ Jesus (Philippians 3:14). Believe Romans 8:28-30.

- Finally, don't live in apprehension that God cannot use or bless you for some vague reason of which you aren't quite sure. Many, many people forget the character of our God. We forget His love, mercy, and grace toward us and instead think of Him as an implacable, rigid, judgmental Father who can never be pleased and who delights to catch us in a fault. How grossly wrong this thinking is!

God looks upon the heart. And if your heart's attitude is to please God, then you have the promise:

> *"Let us therefore, as many as are perfect [mature], have this attitude; and if in anything you have a different attitude, God will reveal that also to you; however, let us keep living by that same standard to which we have attained"* *(Philippians 3:15-16).*

MY RESPONSE TO HIS WORDS...

My Response to His Words...

When You're Worried or Anxious

Do you ever get frustrated or anxious?

It's hard sometimes, isn't it, to have peace when your circumstances are difficult...to have joy when your heart is filled with anxiety?

Circumstances, as well as our frustration and anxiety about the concerns of life, can rob us of our joy.

The apostle Paul was well aware of this as he wrote to the believers at Philippi, for he himself was living under house arrest as a prisoner of the Roman Empire. His circumstances were less than ideal! Yet, listen to his words:

> *"I have learned to be content in whatever circumstances I am. I know how to get along with humble means, and I also know how to live in prosperity; in any and every circumstance I have learned the secret of being filled and going hungry, both of having abundance and suffering need. I can do all things through Him who strengthens me" (Philippians 4:11-13).*

If you'll learn what kept Paul in peace and contentment despite his circumstances, if you'll learn how he handled the anxieties of life, you will have a biblical example and pattern to follow in your own life.

Philippians 4 lays out several precepts which, if adhered to, will grant us the same victory Paul experienced.

First, Paul rejoiced in every circumstance—no matter what it was:

> *"Rejoice in the Lord always; again I will say, rejoice!"*
> *(Philippians 4:4).*

Here is a command that, if obeyed, will bring victory and peace in the midst of any situation. Why? Because the minute you begin rejoicing, your circumstances cease to control you, and you find yourself living above your circumstances as more than a conqueror.

It is crucial to understand, however, that the command to rejoice does not mean rejoicing in your circumstances; it means rejoicing in your Savior who is Lord over every circumstance of life. You could not be in the predicament you are in without the Lord's foreknowledge.

God is sovereign: He rules over all; nothing happens without His permission (Daniel 4:34-35).

Rejoicing is a matter of obedience—an obedience that will start you on the road to peace and contentment.

At this point you may be saying, "But, Kay, I cannot rejoice. I'm just not able! My circumstances are too horrible!"

I understand the overwhelming emotion of such feelings. However, this is where faith enters the picture.

We are to live by faith, not feelings. Then, like Paul, we can handle anything...because of Jesus. Listen to God's Word through the apostle again:

> *"I can do all things through Him who strengthens me"*
> *(Philippians 4:13).*

Or, to paraphrase it: "I can keep on bearing all things through Him who constantly infuses His strength into me."

Christ's strength, His grace, His power are sufficient to enable us to endure whatever comes our way. Therefore, we can "rejoice in the Lord always."

When our circumstances are difficult, it is so easy to get uptight and let this affect our relationships with others. Or we get frustrated and pound things, set them down hard, or slam them! In one way or another we are tempted to vent the frustration of difficult circumstances on a person or an object. Chew out the kids, kick the cat, throw out the dog, hide and glare behind the newspaper, tune out the family and turn on the TV, or slam the bedroom door and pull the blankets over our head.

Yet this is not the way to handle frustration! God wants His children to be different. And so we come to the second precept we need to embrace and obey.

When things are difficult, God says,

> *"Let your gentle spirit be known to all men. The Lord is near" (Philippians 4:5).*

The word translated "gentle" comes from a Greek word difficult to put into English. Some scholars say it could be translated "sweet reasonableness," for it refers to a spirit that doesn't get ruffled and react. In other words, it's an equanimity of spirit that is not affected by circumstances!

The why and wherefore of sweet reasonableness is twofold. One aspect involves requirement; the other involves enablement.

First of all, we *should* act with sweet reasonableness or gentleness because "the Lord is near"—watching, observing, our behavior and our faithful obedience, or lack of it. Then if we look at the phrase from a different perspective, we see that we *are able to* maintain a sweet reasonableness because "the Lord is near"— available to infuse His strength into us!

Isn't that wonderful? He is our everpresent Help in any and every time of need!

In the midst of writing this, we received a phone call that one of our Precept leaders is dying from a type of cancer that has spread from her spine to her esophagus, making it extremely difficult for her to breathe and to talk. I just called her at the hospital in Oklahoma and talked with her and with her precious daughter who is also involved in Precept.

These two women are living examples of what Paul is saying in Philippians 4 regarding joy despite circumstances! As I talked with my dying colaborer about her situation and her imminent death, through labored speech and a choking cough she said, "Kay, I have real contentment and peace. He is all-sufficient. Because I have been in the Word, I can make it. He gives me more grace...real joy and...real peace."

No matter what our circumstances, we can rejoice and let our sweet reasonableness be known to all, receiving from our Lord the power to do so and accepting that power in faith, remembering He is at hand!

But sometimes it isn't a specific circumstance that destroys our joy and our peace. Anxiety about life in general can have the same effect. Do you worry about the fluctuating stock market? The future of our nation? The growing terrorism around the world? Or any number of things that you see around you every day?

Anxiety begins in your mind and, if left unchecked, can frazzle your nerves and eat away at your insides.

Anxiety is a tormentor that can keep you locked in a living hell, immobilizing you so that you cannot cope with life, let alone live as you should for the kingdom of God.

Now the world will tell you that it is natural and normal to be anxious. Well, anxiety may be natural and normal for the world, but it is not to be part of a believer's lifestyle...no matter what our circumstances.

Either God's Word is true, or it is not. Either God is who He says He is, or He's not. And He is who and what He says He is, and His Word stands as His character stands. Therefore, no matter what our future holds, God says,

> *"Be anxious for nothing, but in everything by prayer and supplication with thanksgiving let your requests be made known to God"* (Philippians 4:6).

"Be anxious for nothing" is a command; and yet, in the same breath, God gives us the means of obeying that command.

The moment anxious thoughts invade your mind, go to the Lord in prayer. This is where you begin. The word for prayer is *proseuche,* and it refers to prayer in a general way rather than to petitioning God for specific needs. "General prayer" causes us to look first at God—who He is and what He has promised—rather than at whatever is making us anxious. Focus on God. Rehearse His character, His promises, His works. Remember His names, His attributes, and how they suit your situation. As you rehearse and remember, you will see the cause of your anxiety in a whole new light. Many who have done our devotional study on the names of God, *Lord, I Want to Know You,* have told me that they were able to keep their sanity in the midst of a crisis because they remembered His Name! (Read 2 Chronicles 20 and notice what Jehoshaphat did in a moment of great anxiety.)

After you focus on God in prayer, remembering and rehearsing His character and His promises, then pour out your supplications before your God whom you have just worshiped and adored. The word for supplication is *deesis,* which means "a wanting or a need." It is at this point that you get very specific in your petitions to your God, your Jehovah-jireh, the Lord who provides. Tell God exactly what you want or need. (Watch how Jehoshaphat does this in 2 Chronicles 20.)

Once you have turned your focus on God's character and His promises and have laid your specific petitions regarding your anxieties before His throne, faith is then to take command by giving thanks. Note that Philippians 4:6 says: "By prayer and supplication *with* thanksgiving." The act of thanksgiving is a demonstration of the fact that you are going to trust, to believe God.

> *"Without faith it is impossible to please Him, for he who comes to God must believe that He is [that's where your general prayer comes in] and that He is a rewarder of those who seek Him [this is where supplication comes in]" (Hebrews 11:6).*

The thanksgiving is where the faith comes in.
And what is the end result? Peace instead of anxiety.

"And the peace of God, which surpasses all comprehension, will guard your hearts and your minds in Christ Jesus" (Philippians 4:7).

Much of our anxiety is centered around meeting what we consider the necessities of life. Because of this, many people devote themselves solely—with every ounce of time and energy—to providing these necessities, and luxuries, of life. Then, when the economic situations in their lives take a turn for the worse, or when they are threatened by stock market fluctuations or other financial reverses or uncertainties, anxiety begins to eat away like a cancer. When this happens, it is difficult for them to turn to a God they do not know very well. The ordinary anxieties of life have kept them from the One who promised abundant life!

Oh, my friend, not only do I want you to know these three steps to freedom from anxiety today, but I also want you to be spiritually prepared for tomorrow.

"Do not be anxious about tomorrow" (Matthew 6:34 RSV).

Don't be anxious in the midst of today; and don't be anxious thinking about tomorrow. Know God's Word—and live accordingly.

Invest your time and energies in getting to know your God by getting to know His Word. The returns on that investment are far greater than anything Wall Street has to offer, for these returns— rewards—are eternal.

Trying times are coming, and it is vital that you know how to live. When you do, you won't be anxious about anything!

"No one can serve two masters; for either he will hate the one and love the other, or he will be devoted to one and despise the other. You cannot serve God and wealth. For this reason I say to you, do not be worried about your life....But seek first His kingdom and His righteousness; and all these things will be added to you" (Matthew 6:24-25,33).

MY RESPONSE TO HIS WORDS...

My Response to His Words...

When the World Looks Appealing

Why does life have to be so hard?

Life is hard, and the world's way out is often very appealing. We're tempted—tempted on every hand. People—even many who profess to know Christ—are weakening. And the aftermath is horrible and destructive—to the church, to our nation, to our homes, to our individual lives.

Listen...

"I can't believe God wants me to be so miserable...surely He doesn't want me to be unhappy. Besides, I've had enough...no one can be expected to take what I've taken. I give up. I'm getting out. I'm calling it quits."

...And so over one-half of the marriages in this decade will end in divorce...because someone "can't take it anymore." They "just want to be happy." It doesn't matter that in their pursuit of happiness they have traumatized the lives of their mate and their children.

...And so to justify his or her action, one partner demeans and verbally wounds the other or their children, telling them that it's all their fault. Or in some strange and perverted twist of Scripture, they will bring God in as an advocate to support their sin!

...And so the family buries their heads in their pillows, wetting them with tears until eventually they go to sleep.

...And so the mother has to go to work to support the family, or the abandoned father has to fulfill the role of the mother before he leaves for work.

...And so the children grow up with one parent—one important role model—missing. Often they, in turn, will accept divorce as the reasonable solution to unhappiness because commitment, perseverance, and endurance have not been modeled for them.

And then how will they live?

"But I loved him. He wanted me...We got carried away, but it's all right. We're in love. Besides, everyone's doing it."

...And so she loses her virginity—the one unique gift she could have given her husband.

...And so they had an affair, not believing or knowing that whoever commits fornication sins against his or her own body.

...And so she had an abortion. No sense in bringing an unwanted child into the world.

...And so the seventh commandment is broken.

...And to cover up that one, the sixth commandment is broken.

If happiness isn't sought through relationships, it may be sought through "things."

"If I only had that, I'd be happy...successful...appealing."

At least that is what the media tells us every day. And the lust of the eyes, the lust of the flesh, and the boastful pride of life watch and listen to the advertisements—the appeal of things, success, power....

We're tempted on every hand.

The world is appealing.

Life is hard.

Life is full of disappointments, discouragements, defeats, difficulties.

God's Word calls these "trials." And God says that trials are for our good: They are intended to make us more like Jesus.

But the flesh wants none of this! The flesh doesn't want trials. The flesh doesn't want to suffer or endure hardship.

And so, with every trial there is also the potential of sin. The potential of yielding to the flesh connection. The potential of yielding to temptation.

Listen to the Word of God:

> *"Let no one say when he is tempted, 'I am being tempted by God'; for God cannot be tempted by evil, and He Himself does not tempt anyone. But each one is tempted when he is carried away and enticed by his own lust. Then when lust has conceived, it gives birth to sin; and when sin is accomplished, it brings forth death"* (James 1:13-15).

Whenever we choose not to endure in righteousness but to give way to the flesh, there is a tendency either to blame our circumstances or to blame someone else.

When God confronted Adam with his sin, Adam blamed God for giving Eve to him. Eve blamed the serpent. Neither of them said: "God, I sinned. I yielded to the lust of my eyes, for I saw the fruit and desired it. I yielded to the pride of life, for I knew that it would make me wise. God, I was wrong but I took it."

When you sin, James says, you cannot blame God. God cannot be tempted by evil, and He tempts no one to do evil. Nor can you blame the devil.

Oh, the devil delights to see you sin, but you can't put the blame on him. You cannot say, "The devil made me do it." God says that you sinned because you allowed yourself to be carried along by your own lust, by your own pride, by your own flesh. Satan is the tempter. But he cannot do a thing without your cooperation.

The problem is within—unbridled lust which lures you from obedience to the Word of God. And when lust conceives, it gives birth to sin. And sin kills whatever it touches. Not necessarily physical death. It may be the death of a marriage, a relationship, an opportunity, a ministry, virginity, innocence....Sin kills whatever it touches.

I have heard countless teens testify to what happens to a generation whose parents have yielded to temptation. Our nation and our homes are doomed to destruction—self-destruction—unless we learn to bridle our lust by walking in obedience to the Word of God. Unless we determine to do without, to suffer, even to die rather than disobeying!

Much of this failure is a result of the fact that people either do not know or do not understand the Word of God—or they know and understand but choose not to obey.

> *"Let him who thinks he stands take heed that he does not fall" (1 Corinthians 10:12).*

We must watch and pray, remembering that

> *"no temptation has overtaken you but such as is common to man; and God is faithful, who will not allow you to be tempted beyond what you are able, but with the temptation will provide the way of escape also, so that you will be able to endure it" (1 Corinthians 10:13).*

MY RESPONSE TO HIS WORDS…

My Response to His Words…

When You're Tempted

Have you ever found yourself in a situation where you wanted to take the wrong way out?

Maybe you are weary of the battle—exhausted from trying to do what is right.

Or maybe you feel that no matter how obedient you are, it won't change things anyway.

Maybe you just want to have your own way, like a child throwing a temper tantrum.

Or have things gotten so bad that you simply want to check out?

By that I mean giving up in despair and letting your emotions and thoughts run amuck any which way they want to, rather than allowing the Spirit of God to help you keep them under His control.

Believe me, if you are dealing with any of these temptations, you are not alone. The question is, *How are you dealing with them?*

Many who name the name of Christ choose their own way out of trials and temptations rather than God's way. Our mail at Precept Ministries constantly testifies to this and confirms what awful wreckage and destruction the flesh leaves in the aftermath of having its own way.

And although you may know how to handle the "flesh connection" in trials where yielding to temptation is an ever-present option, I want to share some things that might help you in ministering to your family and to others.

Let me share just part of one out of the thousands of letters we have received crying out for help. This one was sent anonymously as a result of one of our radio broadcasts.

> *How can I live, Kay? I was a virgin bride...years ago. My husband tells me how sweet, precious, and pure I am. I want to vomit. It's not a compliment when it's a lie. I committed adultery but he doesn't know that.*
>
> *I'm guilty, tho' God has forgiven me, I still hurt. My mind is like scrambled eggs and I wonder if I'll ever sort it out again. I wonder if I'll ever stop loving the other man. Will I ever forget his touch, the memories, and the shame and guilt?*
>
> *Warn your listeners that what they think is unbelievable will become reality if they dwell on it. I don't know where it began for me—probably just a thought. My lover had a dream about me a year ago and confessed he dwelt on it till he made it come true. [Elsewhere in the letter, the woman says her former lover was her pastor.]*

Where does sin begin? The book of James gives us the answer.

In the first 12 verses, James talks of trials—the reason God allows them and how we are to handle them. He then closes with a confirmation of God's blessing upon those who persevere rather than taking their own way of escape:

> *"Blessed is a man who perseveres under trial; for once he has been approved, he will receive the crown of life which the Lord has promised to those who love Him"* (James 1:12).

Knowing that some would excuse their lack of perseverance by blaming God for placing the trial and the temptation in their way, James assures us that when we are tempted, we cannot blame God. Listen to what he says about this:

"Let no one say when he is tempted, 'I am being tempted by God'; for God cannot be tempted by evil, and He Himself does not tempt anyone. But each one is tempted when he is carried away and enticed by his own lust. Then when lust has conceived, it gives birth to sin; and when sin is accomplished, it brings forth death. Do not be deceived, my beloved brethren. Every good thing bestowed and every perfect gift is from above, coming down from the Father of lights, with whom there is no variation or shifting shadow" (James 1:13-17).

If we think the source, the hotbed of all temptation is God, then we're deceived. God cannot be tempted by evil, nor does He tempt us.

This is the first thing God wants us to understand. He Himself, because He is God, altogether holy and other than man, would not tempt us to do evil. As a matter of fact, your sovereign God promises you,

"No temptation has overtaken you but such as is common to man; and God is faithful, who will not allow you to be tempted beyond what you are able, but with the temptation will provide the way of escape also, so that you will be able to endure it" (1 Corinthians 10:13).

This, Beloved, is your assurance that God will never permit anything to come your way that you cannot handle. Whatever the trial, testing, or temptation (for that is what the Greek word *peirasmos,* translated "temptation," means), you can know that if it were not possible for you to endure it in a way pleasing to your heavenly Father, then He would not permit it.

Second, God wants you to realize that temptation does not come from without, but from within. Oh, the opportunity to sin is always there, because we live in a world that has been invaded by the evil one, Satan himself. However, it is not the world, nor the devil, which causes you to be tempted—it is your own flesh! What a difference it makes to realize this, for all of a sudden you see your total accountability, and in this day and age that is something few want to acknowledge—*accountability!*

Temptation comes when you are enticed by your own lust. The word for lust is *epithumia* in the Greek, which means "a strong desire of any kind." It can be a good or bad desire, depending on the context in which it is used. The word "enticed" is from a Greek hunting and fishing term meaning "to catch in a snare or trap," or "to lure a fish from behind a rock."

James is very clear here. It's our own lusts—our own desires—that would trap us or lure us away from our God, the Rock (Deuteronomy 32:4). Every desire must be acted upon. It must be denied or fulfilled. It is a matter of choice—ours!

But if a wrong desire is fulfilled, God says that it will bring forth sin, and that sin will bring forth death because sin destroys anything in its path, anything it touches. That death can take many forms—death of innocence, death of an opportunity to serve God, death of purity, death of a relationship.

Sin is a child of desire. Therefore, you need to recognize your desires for what they are. If you rationalize them and accommodate them, you will find yourself in sin. And sin's child is always named Death.

Don't make the deadly mistake of thinking of desires as "needs." God promises to supply all your needs (Philippians 4:19). Needs are never contrary to His Word, but desires are the cravings of your flesh. However, He promises that if you will habitually walk by the Spirit you will not fulfill those desires (Galatians 5:16).

By this, God is not saying that the flesh will not have desires. Rather, He is saying that the flesh and the Spirit "are in opposition to one another" (Galatians 5:17), and because of this tension, you cannot just do as you please. You must consciously choose to walk in the Spirit.

If only the woman who wrote me had immediately denied (put to death) the thoughts (the desires of her flesh) she had about her pastor, she would never had known the awful guilt, shame, pain, and death she is now experiencing.

These two have no one to blame but themselves. And neither do you and I when we give in to temptation. Sin is always the individual's choice and responsibility.

Therefore, I urge you to remember and practice the following:

- Realize that you are never above temptation because it is your own lust—your own flesh—which entices you, and you will have to live with that flesh until the day you die or until the Lord returns.

- Flee from lust. In the power of the Spirit get out of there fast and get far away (2 Timothy 2:22).

- Be careful about the company you keep, for "bad company corrupts good morals" (1 Corinthians 15:33). "Pursue righteousness, faith, love and peace, with those who call on the Lord from a pure heart" (2 Timothy 2:22).

- Acknowledge that in your flesh there dwells no good thing, and "keep watching and praying that you may not enter into temptation," remembering that "the spirit is willing, but the flesh is weak" (Matthew 26:41; see also Romans 7:18 and Matthew 6:13).

- Set your affections on things above; keep eternity before your eyes. Pleasing God is all that is going to matter in the long run.

When you despair in your trial and want to take your own way out, when you long to give up righteousness as a lost cause, when you weary of the pleading of the flesh and want to give in, when you want to let your mind and emotions stampede out of the barn and over the fence of His truths, don't be enticed by your desires, for they will only bring sin and death.

> "Brethren, we are under obligation, not to the flesh, to live according to the flesh—for if you are living according to the flesh, you must die; but if by the Spirit you are putting to death the deeds of the body, you will live. For all who are being led by the Spirit of God, these are sons of God" (Romans 8:12-14).

MY RESPONSE TO HIS WORDS...

My Response to His Words...

When You Face Trials

Have you ever looked at another Christian and thought, "They've got it made! They're so blessed of God!" because they have what you want?

Maybe the person has a great marriage. Maybe she has a husband who loves Jesus. Maybe she has children who love the Lord and desire with all their hearts to serve Him. Or maybe he has the kind of relationship with his children that you long to have, but don't. Maybe he has a successful vocation...or a rewarding ministry. Maybe she has material blessings that have not kept her from loving Jesus. Maybe...well, whatever seems ideal to you...whatever you want so badly but don't have.

Sometimes we look at the goodness of God in someone else's life and wish we could experience the same. Which brings me to my next question.

How often have you heard someone say, "The Lord has been so good to us," as they have shared something good that just happened to them?

I've heard it often...as a matter of fact, from my own lips. And yet, when I say or hear an expression like this, the thought often

crosses my mind, "Would they...would I...have said this if something bad had happened instead?" Would we say, "Such and such
happened...the Lord has been so good to me"?

Probably not.

We seem to associate blessing only with the goodness of God.
However, to do so is to be ignorant of the purpose of the trials—
the difficulties, hardships, and testings—that suddenly invade our
lives (but do not seem to invade the lives of those we envy).

We see trials as robbers, bent on stealing our joy or our sense of
God's blessing and goodness.

How earthbound we are!

How temporal our perspective!

To the child of God, even trials are cause for rejoicing!

> *"Consider it all joy, my brethren, when you encounter*
> *various trials, knowing that the testing of your faith*
> *produces endurance. And let endurance have its perfect*
> *result, that you may be perfect and complete, lacking in*
> *nothing" (James 1:2-4).*

When you encounter a trial, God says, you are to consider it all
joy.

Why?

Because no matter what the trial is, it has a purpose; and that purpose is to make you "perfect and complete, lacking in nothing." The
word for perfect is *teleois,* which means "complete" or "mature"...
in essence, "Christlike."

And because trials are permitted by God, filtered into our lives
through His fingers of love, for the purpose of making us like Jesus,
we can know that no child of God is exempt from trials.

Those who seem so blessed of God, those whom you might have
a tendency to envy, are also going to endure trials if they are genu-
inely His. However, their trials will not necessarily be the same as
yours. In fact, they may be going through trials right now, but you
just don't see it or recognize it.

Do you know why?

Because, Beloved, you are not the same as any other person!
You are uniquely you. So God has a unique, individual set of

circumstances which He will use to refine and purify you so that you will come through the fire of affliction with the dross of your ungodliness consumed.

After Jesus told Peter how He was going to suffer and die, He said to him, "Follow Me!" (John 21:19). Peter, seeing his fellow disciple John, asked Jesus what was going to happen to him. Jesus replied, "What is that to you? You follow Me!" (John 21:22).

According to tradition, Peter was crucified, martyred during the reign of Nero. John was exiled to the Isle of Patmos and later returned to Ephesus, where he was reported to have died a natural death in old age. Yet John was no more blessed by our Lord than Peter. Both men were blessed, and the trials of their faith—unique as they were—were used to make each more like Jesus.

When trials come your way—as inevitably they will—do not run away; and do not be envious of others who seem more blessed of God because they are not enduring what you are experiencing. And don't make the mistake in the midst of your trial of not recognizing the goodness of God in allowing the trial. Consider it all joy!

To consider it all joy is to look past the temporal, down the long road to the eternal...to look beyond the trial to the end result, which is you, perfect and complete, lacking nothing.

Remember, only two things will matter when you see your Lord: how Christlike you have become, and the quality of your work for Him.

Trials are blessings in disguise to get you to that point. If we believe this and act accordingly, we will say with Peter:

> *"In this you greatly rejoice, even though now for a little while, if necessary, you have been distressed by various trials, so that the proof of your faith, being more precious than gold which is perishable, even though tested by fire, may be found to result in praise and glory and honor at the revelation of Jesus Christ" (1 Peter 1:6-7).*

MY RESPONSE TO HIS WORDS...

My Response to His Words...

When You Lack Joy

*Does joy seem to be
a stranger to you?*

Maybe it's because you haven't embraced God's cross in your life. The words of Josif Trif, a 66-year-old Romanian pastor, explain it so clearly: "If it weren't for Communism, I would not have loved our Lord as much. I kissed the cross the Communists gave me."

As you walk through the streets of Romania, you can peer through sparsely stocked storefronts, you can watch people stand in line for hours—sometimes days—to get cheese, bread, a small piece of smelly meat...the barest necessities of life. You can look at their clothes, their cars, their homes, their cities, and you think, "I'm rich! I'm blessed of God!"

But when you listen to their testimonies of the sufficiency of Jesus Christ in the midst of their trials, when you see their joy, you know their kind of joy is joy in spite of circumstances.

And suddenly it hits you. You are poor! They are rich!

Rich because they have known the fellowship of Christ's sufferings! Rich because of a clear conscience—they did not compromise when it would have been expedient and easier to do so! Rich because they embraced the cross with the certain knowledge that Jesus is enough—enough for any trial, for any pain, for any loss.

Tudiose Constantin, a man whose countenance outshines the brilliance of his white hair, wanted us to know that his ten years of imprisonment and his time in a work camp were "the best years of my walk with the Lord. I never felt closer to Him. Now I have a genuine internal desire to do good to my enemies. This is not me, but Jesus in me. I am crucified with Christ, nevertheless I live, yet not me but Christ [Galatians 2:20]."

One dear woman lost her only son in the revolution. He was 26 years old and was to have been married two days later. Can you imagine her sorrow? And the sorrow of his bride-to-be? Can you understand her cross?

Even Romica, whose face and body today bear the scars of leprosy, lights up with joy as he shares his story of months of interrogation. As he lived under the threat of imprisonment, each day he gathered his family and friends for prayer, kissed them good-bye, and reported to the police, wondering if he would ever see his loved ones again. His home had been searched, and everything from toys and candies to books and Bibles—anything religious or not produced in Romania—was confiscated. Finally, his trial came to an end with the revolution!

Later, when Romica asked the Lord why He had permitted all this, the Lord showed him. "I allowed this for two reasons. First, I want you to love the secret police as much as I love them and long to see them in heaven. I wanted you to get to know them. And secondly, because you didn't trust me when I told you not to worry and I gave you Zechariah 10:5: 'They will be as mighty men, treading down the enemy in the mire of the streets in battle; and they will fight, for the LORD will be with them; and the riders on horses will be put to shame.'"

Since the revolution, members of the secret police are greeting Romica openly, and God is giving him the opportunity to share with them because now he knows who they are.

Tudiose and Romica are men who radiate joy because they have embraced the cross of Jesus Christ—as our Lord did, "for the joy set before Him."

O Beloved, if you are lacking joy, it might be because you are failing to walk in the sweetness of faith's obedience, which counts it all joy when it encounters various trials.

Kiss your cross—it's from His sovereign hand. There's a purpose in it all...your Christlikeness. And remember:

> *"Weeping may last for the night, but a shout of joy comes in the morning" (Psalm 30:5b).*

My Response to His Words...

When a Day of Adversity Comes

What is your Goliath?

Are you in a battle? A conflict? A hard place? Is something or someone threatening your peace, your security?

Does a "Goliath" loom before you?

Do you seem so small, so insignificant, so impotent in comparison?

If so, you are looking in the wrong place. Look up! Look up to the heavens, up to your Father's throne, up to your High Priest standing at the right hand of the Father on your behalf.

Then look within! Is the Spirit of the living God not dwelling within? Is He not your resident Helper, your on-call Comforter? Has He not offered you His love, joy, peace, patience, kindness, goodness, faithfulness, gentleness, and self-control?

Nothing has changed! The Father, Son, and Holy Spirit still rule. They are still God. So say to that "Goliath,"

> *"You come to me with a sword, a spear, and a javelin,*
> *but I come to you in the name of the LORD of hosts"*
> *(1 Samuel 17:45).*

God has given you His name—His name which reveals His character and His ways. That's where you are to look.

Look at who God is and what God is.

When David faced Goliath, he remembered that God was *Jehovah-sabaoth, the Lord of hosts,* which means He is the Captain of all—all principalities, powers, and spiritual forces in high places. Every angelic being, good and evil, is under His control! The power and authority belong to God, not to angels or to you or to me.

What is your Goliath? Call upon *Jehovah-nissi, the Lord our Banner!* Run to His camp. Stand under His banner. Call upon the Captain of the hosts.

Can God handle your Goliaths? Of course! David brought Goliath down with a single stone of faith!

Stop and think about it. The other Israelites had the same God on their side that David had on his! Then what made the difference? David trusted in what He knew about God. Saul, Israel's king, tried to dress David in his armor, to equip him with his sword. Saul was trusting in the arm of flesh. David knew that the weapons of his warfare were not fleshly but mighty through God.

Oh, Beloved, don't you see? God in His sovereignty permits "Goliaths" in your life as tests...tests which give you an opportunity to prove your faith. And in proving your faith, you prove Him and, thus, are strengthened.

David had been strengthened by his previous encounters with lions and bears. God had delivered him then; He could do it again. The lions and bears were preparation for Goliath!

You'll never be the Christian you can be without "Goliaths." You'll never know God intimately apart from them. It's the trials, the conflicts, the adversities, the "no way out" situations, the impossibilities that drive us to God, where we discover who He is and what He is.

Not to run to Him means to miss knowing Him and experiencing His power, His glory, His majesty, His sufficiency.

When the king of Aram surrounded the city where the prophet Elisha was staying, the king was furious because Elisha had kept revealing his battle plans to the king of Israel. So he sent horses, chariots, and a great army to get one man—Elisha! When Elisha's servant saw the army encircling the city, he cried out to the prophet, "Alas, my master! What shall we do?" And Elisha answered:

> *"Do not fear, for those who are with us are more than those who are with them" (2 Kings 6:16).*

Then Elisha prayed for his servant, " 'O LORD, I pray, open his eyes that he may see.' And the LORD opened the servant's eyes and he saw; and behold, the mountain was full of horses and chariots of fire all around Elisha" (2 Kings 6:17).

The Lord of hosts, Jehovah-sabaoth, was there all the time. The king of Aram's army was struck blind!

I pray that our *El Roi, the God who sees,* will open your eyes that you might see that He is always there with His very real but unseen hosts to move on your behalf.

I pray that you will begin to meet every "Goliath" in that confidence.

I pray that you'll get to know your God by name, and that in the day of adversity you'll not hesitate to call upon the name of the Lord, that you'll not hesitate to run "into His name" and be secure.

> *"Woe to those who go down to Egypt [the world] for help and rely on horses, and trust in chariots because they are many and in horsemen because they are very strong, but they do not look to the Holy One of Israel, nor seek the LORD!" (Isaiah 31:1).*

Seek Him. Look to Him. Cling to His truth. You will not be disappointed!

> *"The LORD also will be a stronghold for the oppressed, a stronghold in times of trouble; and those who know Your name will put their trust in You, for You, O LORD, have not forsaken those who seek You" (Psalm 9:9-10).*

My Response to His Words...

When It Seems Nothing Will Ever Change

Is there really any chance for a new direction in our lives?

Is there any chance of turning around a marriage that's becoming nothing more than a cold war?

Is there any chance of victoriously dealing with the loss of a child's affection?

Is there any chance of letting go of the bitterness of a wounded relationship, a disappointing past?

Is there any chance of changing the drudgery you face each day as you go to work?

Is there any chance of changing the morals of our decadent society?

Is there any chance of coming out of depression or defeat and actually looking forward to the days ahead?

Is there any chance of being assured that you're being used of God so that when your life is over, you'll know that it hasn't been in vain? So that you'll know, whether others recognize it or not, that your life has had eternal merit?

There's not only a chance but a certain assurance if you will do one thing: if you will embrace the cross.

While living at the cross may not change the circumstances or the other parties involved in your situations, you will find that at the cross there will be change—change that has eternal significance and merit.

In general, however, we hear very little about the cross.

We hear more about the crown, and we want to wear it now!

Or we look at those who seem to be wearing crowns—perhaps because they're popular, or they draw crowds, or are hailed by man—and we think, "Man, they've got it made! They must be doing something right. I think I'll follow them!"

But before you move on those suppositions, before you start following, check out their relationship to the cross of Jesus Christ.

Just after Peter made his awesome confession that Jesus was the Christ (Messiah), the Son of the living God, Jesus told the disciples that He was going to Jerusalem to suffer many things, to be killed, and that He would be raised from the dead.

Peter replied to this statement from Jesus by proclaiming, "God forbid it, Lord! This shall never happen to You."

With that, Jesus turned to Peter and said, "Get behind Me, Satan! You are a stumbling block to Me; for you are not setting your mind on God's interests, but man's."

Then Jesus said to His disciples, "If anyone wishes to come after Me, he must deny himself, and take up his cross and follow Me" (Matthew 16:21-24).

When you stop to study and think about this passage, you see two philosophies: Satan's (and thus the world's) and then God's.

Satan, who is the prince of this world, used Peter's mouth to say, "Spare yourself, take care of yourself, look out for 'number one.'"

Jesus says we are to do just the opposite. We are to deny ourselves, to die to self—even though it's painful. The cross was an excruciating method of death, a prolonged one.

Satan said, "Live."

Jesus said, "Die."

Satan appeals to the flesh and the logic of the world.

Jesus calls us to the Spirit's resurrection power that comes only when we die. The cross flies in the face of the world's wisdom, because the cross is the power of God. Even at His weakest moment on Calvary, Jesus was stronger than men. (Read 1 Corinthians 1:18-31).

Who will you listen to?

You know which one is easier to listen to and, thus, to believe— the one who offers you a temporary crown! But you also know, don't you, that Satan is a murderer, a liar, a deceiver? He doesn't abide in the truth because there's no truth in him (John 8:44).

The life you long for, the changes you want, come only through the cross—no other way. If you will live at the cross, the cross will take care of the past. This is the message of Romans 6. This is why Paul said:

> *"I have been crucified with Christ; and it is no longer I who live, but Christ lives in me; and the life which I now live in the flesh I live by faith in the Son of God, who loved me and gave Himself up for me" (Galatians 2:20).*

The cross will take care of the flesh, that ugly Goliath that threatens, torments, and taunts you. The flesh that drags you down, that wants its rights, that cries out for justice, vengeance, and recompense. The flesh that says, "When you meet my needs, I'll meet yours." The flesh that bids you flee the cross as it convinces you it is too much to bear. The flesh that refuses reconciliation unless it comes on its own terms.

Jesus told us to take up our cross and die daily. Paul said that those who belong to Christ have crucified the flesh with all its passions and desires (Galatians 5:24). Only in this way will we control the flesh.

The cross takes care of the world with its lusts and boastful pride.

The cross is God's message of victory to the world that we are not only to proclaim with our lips, but underline with our lives. It is the path of ministry.

Read the following words from John 12 carefully, prayerfully. Don't just glance over them, for this is the means of change, my friend.

> *"And Jesus answered them saying, 'The hour has come for the Son of Man to be glorified. Truly, truly, I say to you, unless a grain of wheat falls into the earth and dies, it remains alone; but if it dies, it bears much fruit. He who loves his life loses it, and he who hates his life in this world will keep it to life eternal. If anyone serves Me, he must follow Me; and where I am, there My servant will be also; if anyone serves Me, the Father will honor him.*
>
> *" 'Now My soul has become troubled; and what shall I say, "Father, save Me from this hour"? But for this purpose I came to this hour. Father, glorify Your name.' Then a voice came out of heaven: 'I have both glorified it, and will glorify it again.' So the crowd of people who stood by and heard it were saying that it had thundered; others were saying, 'An angel has spoken to Him.' Jesus answered and said, 'This voice has not come for My sake, but for your sakes. Now judgment is upon this world; now the ruler of this world will be cast out. And I, if I am lifted up from the earth, will draw all men to Myself.' But He was saying this to indicate the kind of death by which He was to die" (John 12:23-33).*

Jesus came for this hour, the hour of crucifixion. And where would we be had He chosen the crown offered by Satan when he promised Jesus all the kingdoms of the world if He would worship him?

If Jesus had spared Himself, you and I would never have been able to be changed. We would have been trapped eternally in our sin and all its formidable, eternal, destructive consequences.

But because He embraced the cross, you and I can be changed forever.

And, Beloved, if you will embrace your cross, your life will have an eternal impact. A crucified life cannot help but change things...and people.

When we live at the cross, crucified with Christ, we are living life to its fullest because we're living by faith.

When we live by faith—at the cross—life with all its problems, disappointments, frustrations, and pressures takes on a whole new—glorious—perspective. Nothing is more important than pleasing Him. And when we've truly pleased Him, we can leave everything at the foot of His cross.

There's room at the cross. May we live there together.

> *"May it never be that I would boast, except in the cross of our Lord Jesus Christ, through which the world has been crucified to me, and I to the world"* (Galatians 6:14).

My Response to His Words...

When Divorce
Seems Like an Option

---

*Has there ever been a time, even for
a second, when you have thought it
might be nice to be divorced?*

Perhaps you think your mate is not meeting your needs. Perhaps you have an unbelieving mate.

However, if you ever, even for a second, entertain such a thought, you need to stop and ask God what His perspective is in the subject of divorce. You will soon find that He feels passionately about the subject.

How I appreciate those who are living with mates who are talking divorce and who want to know what God says about it in His Word.

How I wish that those who profess to be His children would consult His Word to see what His heart is on the subject before they even begin to entertain the thought of leaving their mate.

Before we focus our attention on what God has to say on the subject, however, I feel that I need to say a word to those of you who are already divorced.

I know that there are many of you who never desired a divorce, who hate being divorced, and who, as a result of being the unwilling party, find yourself divorced and thereby feel like a second-class citizen in the family of God.

Oh, dear one, don't heap upon yourself a condemnation that is not from God.

Although other people may not understand, remember that all things are naked and open in the sight of God, and someday those things that are hidden now will be revealed for what they are. God will justify the innocent and clear those unjustly declared guilty by man.

Therefore, as you read what God says in the book of Malachi, do not add to or take away from His words. Hear His heart:

> "'This is another thing you do: you cover the altar of the LORD with tears, with weeping and with groaning, because He no longer regards the offering or accepts it with favor from your hand. Yet you say, "For what reason?" Because the LORD has been a witness between you and the wife of your youth, against whom you have dealt treacherously, though she is your companion and your wife by covenant....Take heed then...and let no one deal treacherously against the wife of your youth. 'For I hate divorce,' says the LORD, the God of Israel"* (Malachi 2:13-16).

Do you know why God hates divorce?

For two definite reasons.

First, because, as Malachi mentions, marriage is a covenant, and covenants are not to be broken.

God made a covenant with Israel, and because of it, Israel was not forsaken. God is a covenant-keeping God.

God also made a covenant with the church, His bride, His body. That covenant is the new covenant in His blood which grants us grace that leads to eternal life.

God hates divorce because it is the breaking of a covenant.

Second, God hates divorce because marriage is a picture of our covenant union with the Lord Jesus Christ.

Earthly marriages are to be a picture of our heavenly marriage to Him. So God hates divorce because it distorts His eternal commitment to us: He will never leave us or forsake us.

Think on it, Beloved...and never entertain the thought again.

> "The lovingkindness of the Lord is from everlasting to
>   everlasting on those who fear Him,
> And His righteousness to children's children,
> To those who keep His covenant
> And remember His precepts to do them" (Psalm
>   103:17-18).

My Response to His Words...

When You're Tempted to Tolerate Evil

How much do you hate evil? Do you ever whitewash it? Excuse it?

Or, for the approval of others, do you tolerate evil in their lives? Do you even call evil good?

We live in a time of great tolerance of evil.

Black is not black.

White is not white.

Gray is the color of choice when it comes to moral issues. Color everything gray—all shades, depending on your tolerance of darkness or light.

Even some Christians think, "Just don't make the issues black or white; no absolutes, please. Absolutes are rigid, cramping, distasteful, and intolerant! There is a little bit of good in everyone, and we need to see the good. After all, God does!"

Oh, does He?

Thinking, or should I say, rationalizing like that wearies God. It is an assault against His character and His Word.

Listen to what He says to us in the book of Malachi:

> *"You have wearied the* LORD *with your words. Yet you say, 'How have we wearied Him?' In that you say, 'Everyone who does evil is good in the sight of the* LORD, *and He delights in them,' or, 'Where is the God of justice?'"* (Malachi 2:17).

The phrase "where is the God of justice?" implies that God is not going to judge sin. After all, where is He?

To which God replies,

> *"'Behold, I am going to send My messenger, and he will clear the way before Me. And the Lord, whom you seek, will suddenly come to His temple; and the messenger of the covenant, in whom you delight, behold, He is coming,' says the* LORD *of hosts. 'But who can endure the day of His coming? And who can stand when He appears? For He is like a refiner's fire'"* (Malachi 3:1-2).

In other words, the Lord says, "I am coming, and who can endure the day of My coming?" For when He comes, He "will draw near to you for judgment" and will be

> *"a swift witness against the sorcerers and against the adulterers and against those who swear falsely, and against those who oppress the wage earner in his wages, the widow and the orphan, and those who turn aside the alien and do not fear Him"* (Malachi 3:5).

Compromising men and women may call evil good in the sight of the Lord and say that God delights in them, but that is a lie. God never compromises with evil; He only exposes evil for what it is and then judges it.

Jehoshaphat was a great king who sought the God of his fathers, sending forth His officials so that

> *"they taught in Judah, having the book of the law of the* LORD *with them; and they went throughout all the cities of Judah and taught among the people"* (2 Chronicles 17:9).

Yet there came a time when righteous Jehoshaphat made an alliance with ungodly Ahab, king of Israel. It was this alliance that brought a severe rebuke from God through Jehu, when he said to Jehoshaphat:

> *"Should you help the wicked and love those who hate the* LORD *and so bring wrath on yourself from the* LORD*?" (2 Chronicles 19:2).*

Good question, isn't it?

And how would you answer it, Beloved?

What is your alliance with the ungodly?

And what is your allegiance to them?

Your only allegiance ought to be the love of God that would mourn over their sin and seek to rescue them from the certain flames of judgment which shall torment the wicked forever.

However, to align with them or with their evil is to incur the judgment of God.

Remember that! You serve a holy God.

> *"Holy, Holy, Holy, is the* LORD *of hosts,*
> *The whole earth is full of His glory" (Isaiah 6:3).*

My Response to His Words…

When You Are Tempted to Complacency

Have you ever wondered if there's any hope of being the man or woman of God you've longed to be...or know you should be?

Does it seem like a goal too far away to be reached? So high that you could never reach it? An ambition that is attainable only by supersaints, but not by someone like you?

At the same time that I ask that question, may I ask another that may seem totally unrelated...but isn't? My second question is, "Have you ever wondered whether or not there is any hope for America?"

I have. Every time I watch television (which fortunately is not often), every time I pick up a magazine, every time I read the headlines in the newspapers, I think, *Father, I've heard it all. We can't sink any lower...we've reached the pit of degradation.*

Let me share some statistics of what is happening to the children in America. Don't read these lightly—these things are happening to real children. Your child or grandchild could be one of them!

Every 24 hours...

- 4,342 children are arrested
- 3,544 babies are born to unmarried mothers
- 2,911 high-school students drop out
- 1,354 babies are born to teen mothers
- 351 children are arrested for drug abuse
- 186 children are arrested for violent crimes
- 10 children and youth under 20 are homicide victims
- 6 children and youth under 20 commit suicide
- 1 young person under 25 dies from HIV infection*

Add to these statistics the militant boldness of the homosexuals and the pedophiles and the ever-increasing spread of pornography, and you should realize that if God had to judge Sodom and Gomorrah and the children of Israel, He must surely judge America.

In Ezekiel 22 the word of the Lord came to the prophet Ezekiel telling him to make known to Jerusalem all of its abominations—abominations which God would have to judge.

In this chapter Jerusalem is described as a bloody city because of all that had occurred within its walls: oppression of the fatherless, widows, and children; lewdness; adultery; incest; murder; graft and corruption; idolatry; robbery; oppression.

Prophets and priests had succumbed to greed and corruption. The priests had ceased to distinguish between the clean and the unclean. The prophets were telling the people what they wanted to hear rather than exposing their sin for what it was and calling the people to repentance.

And instead of seeking the welfare of the nation, the leaders of Israel were shedding blood and destroying lives in order to get dishonest gain.

---

* Excerpted from Children's Defense Fund Web site (http://www.childrensdefense.org/everyday.htm). Used with permission. ©2001 Children's Defense Fund.

Israel's cup of iniquity was full, and God had to move in judg-ment...yet, He didn't want to. Over and over He had called them to repentance, but they would not listen to the voice of God's prophets.

Can you not hear the anguish in His voice as He says:

> *"I searched for a man among them who would build up the wall and stand in the gap before Me for the land, so that I would not destroy it; but I found no one" (Ezekiel 22:30).*

"I searched...but I found no one." Tragic, isn't it? And so God goes on to say:

> *"'Thus I have poured out My indignation on them; I have consumed them with the fire of My wrath; their way I have brought upon their heads,' declares the Lord GOD" (Ezekiel 22:31).*

You have heard that prayer can change things. But have you ever realized that God could use your earnest prayers to change the course of our nation's history, to stay God's hand of judgment, *and* to make you into the child of God you long to be in the process? For you cannot spend time in prayer—even intercessory prayer—and not have it impact you personally.

I urge you to take these matters to the Lord. See how the Spirit speaks to your heart. Pray for our land. Ask the Lord to create within you a sense of urgency and to cause you to cry for a greater degree of holiness.

- Get your mind off yourself and think of God.

- Ask Him to teach you how to intercede.

- Plead for the leaders of our land.

- Pray that men and women will turn from their wickedness and bow in godly sorrow and repen-tance.

- Plead for God's mercy on our land.

Plead for God's deliverance, and plead for His children. Plead for His Spirit to be poured out upon our land. Plead that He will rain holiness upon the land.

If you'll begin to pray diligently in this way and ask God to give you clean hands and a pure heart, then God will use your intercession to make you more like the man or woman of God you long to be. You can't be in His presence praying like this and not have it change you!

And if we all diligently intercede for our nation, perhaps He will stay His hand of judgment and bring revival.

Lay down the spirit of complacency. Now is not the time to be sleeping. Now is the time to use our weapons of warfare. Clothe yourself in His armor and take up the weapons He has given you and fight. Fight...

> *" 'not by might nor by power, but by My Spirit,' says the* LORD *of hosts" (Zechariah 4:6).*

My Response to His Words...

When You're Tempted
Not to Share the Gospel

Have you almost given up hope on certain people?

Have you wondered if...or how...God could ever turn them around because they have been so deeply involved in sin?

Let me share a story which I believe will not only encourage and bless you, but also prod you to pray without ceasing and to share the gospel without shame or hesitation.

"From *Penthouse* to Precept!" Those are the words scrawled across the white notebook paper bearing the testimony of a woman who came to our Precept Leadership Training. How I pray that my friend's story will encourage you to persevere in prayer for your wayward sons and daughters. You never know how God is at work.

> *After college, I went to work for* Penthouse *and* Viva *magazines as Assistant Public Relations Director, handling national press tours for the contributing writers, editor, and the models. It seemed to be the perfect job for me. Right out of college—exciting, meeting famous people,*

traveling, writing. I also wrote the in-house advertising copy for the magazine. (Ick!) And it was daring and naughty, too.

That I went to church every Sunday, and even visited churches on the Sunday I was on the road for Penthouse, *never even struck me as paradoxical. My mainline church never really addressed sin other than generally. My idea was that to sin was to hurt someone else.*

The university I attended actually encouraged and taught sensuality. I was directed to have sexual relationships by a counselor there to "release" me "from my hang-ups" and to help me "grow up." So my job at Penthouse *seemed perfect. Except that after two years, I was weighted down.*

Something was wrong; it wasn't fun anymore. These people were too serious about others following what they believed. They actually advocated use of these publications in counseling therapy. When I told them how I felt, I came under immediate disfavor.

My spirit was in torment. The Holy Spirit was starting to draw me. I went on a spiritual retreat where reflection led me to the knowledge that I needed to make a change—the beginning of a long journey through days as an actress (seeing things that sickened my spirit regarding mysticism, homosexuality, all kinds of sensual perversions!) and days in marketing for Hawaiian Tropic *where one Christian shone like a light. I asked him why and prayed "the sinner's prayer" with him.*

There followed days in advertising and public relations for concerns in Florida and finally—two-and-one-half years later—real conversion!—really, completely offering myself—all of me—to the Lord at age 28.

God is so good. He has sent me teachers and disciplers since—a lot of them right away—and I grew quickly. But now, seven years later, He has led me into really seeking maturity in Him, and He is providing lavishly for this growth.

> *God is using Precept as a primary tool in shaping me—giving me biblical grounding like I'd never had before and never knew was possible. This digging for knowledge and application of that knowledge is so exciting, so strengthening.*
>
> *It's like a tree starting out as a spindly, bendy, little sapling, adding rings and rings of growth as it matures into a magnificent oak with roots reaching deep into the earth, giving it stability in its strength and growth.*
>
> *All of this as I try to be the wife, mommy, and now the teacher God wants me to be. He has transformed me and I am now using my mind, my skills, my mouth for Him and not for the flesh of the world. I praise and thank Him for that....*

Oh, Beloved, as I read that, I think of two verses:

> *"You will know the truth, and the truth will make you free" (John 8:32).*

> *"Sanctify them in the truth; Your word is truth" (John 17:17).*

But how can they hear the truth unless someone cares enough to share it?

I cannot tell you how often I have shared the gospel with someone sitting next to me on a plane and thought *Their grandparents, mother, father, or wife would be so excited if only they knew how their prayers are being answered right now.* I say this because many times when I have shared the gospel, these individuals have told me of originally hearing it from just such a loved one.

You may not see it—but God is at work. He has a Father's heart; the world is on His heart. But He needs men and women who are equipped and established in His Word and not ashamed of the gospel of Jesus Christ, for it is the power of God unto salvation to everyone who believes. But how can they believe in Someone they have never heard of? And how can they hear unless we tell them?

We must awake from our apathetic sleep, arise from our self-centered entanglements, stand for Christ, get established in His Word, and get involved in making disciples.

Our time is short—shorter than we think. And we can't take anything with us when this life is over—except the souls we have invested in.

Think on it—and pray, "God, what would You have me to do? Who and what am I to pray for? With whom am I to share Your gospel?"

> *"I solemnly charge you in the presence of God and of Christ Jesus, who is to judge the living and the dead, and by His appearing and His kingdom: preach the word; be ready in season and out of season; reprove, rebuke, exhort, with great patience and instruction"* *(2 Timothy 4:1-2).*

My Response to His Words...

When You Watch
Our Foundations Crumble

---

*Have you noticed the changes in
the morals of our country during the
past years?*

When I flipped the television dial to CNN and caught a report on what they were doing on the Berkeley campus with condoms, something happened inside me.

Oh Father, I thought, *we have gone too far! We have hit the depths of sin! There's no turning back!*

When I turned on *Nightline* and saw what the BBC had produced in reaction to cases of AIDS reported in England, my body was racked with sobs as I went to the Lord in prayer. I could not believe that the British—or anyone for that matter—could so blatantly describe what a person should do in order to avoid AIDS without ever once dealing with the issue of morality.

When I picked up an issue of *Newsweek* and read an article on "Kids and Contraceptives," my heart ached as I noted the following:

The teen pregnancy rate is dramatically higher in the United States than in other Western nations....Recalling a scene from a national television program...when a boy's mother finds his contraceptives, in a heart-to-heart talk she says, "Just make sure whatever you do, it is the right time in your life."

Things are changing, and they are changing very rapidly. And in the midst of these changes, there's confusion, there's chaos, there's conflict.

The very foundations of our society are crumbling. If we are going to survive the holy judgment of God—which is here in part and yet is to come in greater measure—then you need to do two things:

First, you need to know what never changes. It is God and His Word.

God is the same yesterday, today, and forever. He will never change; His character will never change. And it is because of this that God, in His righteousness, will have to judge our iniquity. America cannot continue the way it is going without experiencing the just judgment of God.

God cannot alter the Word which has gone out from His lips. What God has said must come to pass.

"Do not be deceived; neither fornicators, nor idolaters, nor adulterers, nor effeminate, nor homosexuals, nor thieves, nor the covetous, nor drunkards, nor revilers, nor swindlers, will inherit the kingdom of God. Such were some of you; but you were washed, but you were sanctified, but you were justified in the name of the Lord Jesus Christ, and in the Spirit of our God....

"Do you not know that your bodies are members of Christ? Shall I then take away the members of Christ and make them members of a prostitute? May it never be!...Flee immorality. Every other sin that a man commits is outside the body, but the immoral man sins against his own body. Or do you not know that your body is a temple of the Holy Spirit who is in you, whom you have from God, and that you are not your own? For

> *you have been bought with a price: therefore glorify*
> *God in your body" (1 Corinthians 6:9-11,15,18-20).*

This is what we are failing to share with our world, and we must share it. God has set us as watchmen upon the wall, and if we as His children see God's sword of judgment coming and do not warn the people, the sword will surely come, but their blood shall be upon our hands:

> *"Son of man, I have appointed you a watchman to the*
> *house of Israel; whenever you hear a word from My*
> *mouth, warn them from Me" (Ezekiel 3:17).*

Our young people need a wholesome dose of the "fear of God" in them, as does the rest of our nation—"the fear of the LORD is to hate evil" (Proverbs 8:13).

Oh, Beloved, where are the watchmen to sound God's trumpet and warn the people? What are you doing as His watchman on the wall to let people know who God is and what His Word says? May I make some suggestions?

- Pray consistently for the moral situation in our nation. Ask God to bring us to a godly sorrow that will lead to repentance.

- Put godly pressure on your PTAs and city officials to present what God says about our sexuality. Josh McDowell has an excellent video series, "Why Wait?" and Precept Ministries has one called "Sex, Teens, and Dating." If the PTAs will not permit this, work through the churches or plan some citywide campaigns.

- Write letters to the newspapers and the city officials. Let your voice be heard—but let it be heard in the firmness and graciousness of our Lord. Do not be nasty or rude. Know what you are talking about. Get the facts, or you will wound yourself and the body of Christ.

- Try to get on television and radio—local news or talk shows. When you do, remember you have only one weapon because that is all you need. It is the Word of God. Just keep saying sweetly but firmly, "But God's Word says...." Remember, His Word is alive, powerful, and sharper than any two-edged sword. Use it. It is all you need.

- Buy airtime and use the videos mentioned above or your own programs that present what God's Word has to say on sexuality.

- Write and print attractive and well-done materials that will spell out what God says about immorality and its consequences. Go to businesses in your city (begin with Christian businesspeople) and get them to help you finance and distribute the materials.

- Find out what your local laws are regarding pornography and places where immorality is sold in one form or another. Then gather a group of godly or moral citizens and take proper legal action to stop what is going on. Support these actions with a strong base of warfare praying, and do not quit until you have the victory. Some cities have been rid of immoral places through just such actions, and it can happen in your city if you will do your part.

- Get your local pastors or their representatives together and prayerfully seek what God would have you do. Then do it without fail.

Second, you need to walk in complete and total obedience to God's Word. No compromise!

The world is looking for people who really believe and live what they say. And that is exactly the problem with much of the professing church of Jesus Christ, isn't it? We honor Him with our lips, but our hearts are far from Him. For if we really loved Him, we would keep His commandments.

Our marriages, our families, our churches, our society, our morals are crumbling. The pure, unadulterated Word of God is what our nation needs.

Remember, you are God's watchman on the wall!

> *"Be on guard for yourselves and for all the flock, among which the Holy Spirit has made you overseers, to shepherd the church of God which He purchased with His own blood" (Acts 20:28).*

My Response to His Words...

When Life Doesn't Follow Your Plan

How do you handle disappointment?

Disappointment. It's like a cloud that suddenly separates you from the warmth of the Son.

A chill overcomes you and you shudder. Drawing your arms tighter around yourself doesn't help.

You hurt. Yet it is not a physical pain.

It's hard to concentrate...hard to listen to what others are saying because all you can think of is the disappointment that has intruded into your world.

There can be all sorts of reasons for disappointments, but one thing is certain: You are disappointed because something has happened that is not in accord with your desire or not in accord with your plan.

Disappointment can come because of the behavior of someone else...because of a certain alteration in your circumstances... because your plans or desires have suddenly been thwarted... because something didn't turn out the way you hoped or expected...because something you once had is gone.

How do you handle disappointment so that you are not over-whelmed...demolished...demoralized? So that you don't give up? So that you don't walk away from life thinking, *Well, it's all over now. I'll never be the same. I'll never have what I've wanted. I've missed it. It's gone...forever, gone.*

You handle it, my friend, by understanding that *disappointment is God's appointment.*

Disappointment is a trial of your faith...a test that proves the genuineness of your relationship with your God and His Word.

Disappointment is something which, strange as it may seem, has been filtered through God's sovereign fingers of love. He has allowed disappointment to slip through His fingers into your life, which He holds in the palm of His omnipotent hand.

Disappointment is something that God has deemed necessary in order to bring you to His goal—Christlikeness and fruitfulness.

This is why God had James pen the following words:

> *"Consider it all joy, my brethren, when you encounter various trials, knowing that the testing of your faith produces endurance. And let endurance have its perfect result, that you may be perfect and complete, lacking in nothing" (James 1:2-4).*

To "consider it all joy" sounds a little insane, perhaps even masochistic. Why consider it all joy when you are overwhelmed with pain, captured by disappointment?

Because, my friend, your God commands it. And He commands it because your obedient response will be the making of you.

If the disappointment, the trial, were not for your benefit and His glory, He would never have allowed it to seep through His fingers into your life. Not because He desires to hurt you, make you miserable, demoralize you, ruin your life, or keep you from ever knowing happiness. Rather, it is because He wants you to have every opportunity to be Christlike and fruitful. God doesn't want you to have any regrets when you see Him face-to-face.

Disappointments are God's appointments. He allows them to seep through His fingers, for in His omniscience God knows their end result will be for our good and His glory.

How well I remember the day I faced one of the biggest disappointments of my Christian life. It was the day, more than thirty years ago, when my husband, Jack, took me off the mission field.

For three-and-a-half years we had lived in Guadalajara, Mexico, where Jack assisted other missionaries through film evangelization and literature distribution while I worked with English-speaking teens, being used of God to bring them to salvation and then to disciple them through the Word. Plus, I made mission trips out to remote villages where I would use my nursing skills to minister to people who were so needy—spiritually and physically.

I loved Mexico. It was home to me. And I knew that once our youngest son was old enough, I would be able to spend more time working with the Mexican people and would finally have an opportunity to learn Spanish.

But it never happened.

Suddenly, I was confined to my bed with a heart condition, allowed out once a day, and then only as far as the bathroom.

A trip to the States and a doctor's recommendation to leave Mexico was all that it took for Jack to pack us up and move us back to the States.

Disappointment hit.

I wept. I grieved. I agonized in prayer, crying out to God. I felt that I had failed Him. I had taken a much-needed man off the mission field. I had brought Jack's missionary career of thirteen years to a halt through my physical weakness. For weeks I lived in torment of mind and heart, for I did not see my disappointment as His appointment.

Peace came only when I slipped to the floor one morning and, there on my knees, finally surrendered my expectations, evaluations, desires, and said, "Father, whatever You want."

With that the tide turned. Jack was asked to build and manage a new radio station in Chattanooga, and I began to work with teens from our church. Soon afterward I also began teaching a women's Bible study as well as a Bible study for college students on the University of Tennessee at Chattanooga campus.

But what of Mexico? What of my desire to minister on foreign fields? What of my disappointment in this respect?

It would take about twenty-one years for me to see with my own eyes, to hear with my own ears what God was about when He took us to Mexico only to bring us home after three-and-a-half years. God's ways, as I would see with hindsight, were far greater than mine...much higher. The heart of longing He had given us for the Mexican people was not in vain...it was simply to be fulfilled in a far greater, more extensive way than my little mind could ever imagine.

Twenty-one years after we left, Jack and I returned to Mexico for nine days of ministry in Mexico City. During those days we met with, prayed with, sang with, and ministered with the leaders of our Precept Ministries there, "Precepto Sobre Precepto." Many of these leaders were pastors, and we heard testimony after testimony of how Precept had been the means of building their churches, of the ability people now had to study God's Word for themselves, and of how it had transformed their lives! Over and over we heard that this study method is what Latin America has needed, for there is no other material in Spanish that is accomplishing what Precept is accomplishing.

We saw over 120 people indicate that they were repenting and receiving Jesus Christ as their Lord and Savior. Men and women, young and old, rich and poor responded after attending classes where they were clearly taught the gospel and what the Word says about salvation. It meant so much to us, too, when these dear people embraced us, kissed us, patted us, and told us that now they were equipped for ministry. Even missionaries told us how God had used Precept to change their lives!

What Jack and I could never have done had we continued as we were in Mexico, God had done through a great disappointment to me. But it took over twenty years before He revealed what He had in mind for me when He brought us home. I simply had to come to the point where I would obey His command and in my disappointment count it all joy—knowing, but not seeing, that if I would endure and remain steadfast in my faith, He would use it to make me more like Christ and to accomplish His perfect will.

"Having been justified by faith, we have peace with God through our Lord Jesus Christ, through whom

also we have obtained our introduction by faith into this grace in which we stand; and we exult in hope of the glory of God. And not only this, but we also exult in our tribulations, knowing that tribulation brings about perseverance; and perseverance, proven character; and proven character, hope; and hope does not disappoint, because the love of God has been poured out within our hearts through the Holy Spirit who was given to us" (Romans 5:1-5).

My Response to His Words...

Words of
TRUST

When Your Heart Aches

Have you ever had to deal with a recurring heartache?

Maybe it's something from your past. Maybe it's something you are having to live through right now. But whether past or present, it weighs heavily. Life seems harder. The hurt and heaviness hang like a dark cloud between you and joy.

You want to cry...but you know if you do it might go on for days. And although tears might relieve the pressure, you know they wouldn't change a thing.

You wish you could write it off...or, if it's a person, you wish you could just forget them. But despite the tears, the pain, the torture, you can't seem to let go.

Sometimes running away from the heartache seems attractive, but would running away really solve it?

You look at others...they seem so happy.

You sigh wistfully and wish things had been different
    in your life
    in your situation
    in your relationships
    in your experiences.

You wish you had known better,
    had done differently.
Others seem to have what you would like to have...
    in their relationships
    in their circumstances of life....
Emotionally, materially, spiritually, physically, intellectually, professionally...you feel: "They won...and I lost."

Maybe because you smile, no one knows.

Maybe because you cover up, no one suspects.

Maybe because you are silent, no one can share, relate, and give you hope.

So you feel locked away in loneliness...and your heart hurts.

The happiness of others only makes your pain worse. It shouldn't. You want to rejoice for them, but you can't. You hurt too much.

Sometimes you may even have to deal with envy...with jealousy...or with grief...or anger...or depression...or wanting to die.

I do understand, Beloved, because at one time or another I have had to deal with all of this. And more and more as I read our mail, I know I am not alone. Christians are not exempt from heartache.

Yet, though not exempt, we do have the means to endure heartache without falling apart!

For this we have Jesus...His grace, His sufficiency.

For this we have His Word...His promises, His wisdom.

If I did not know that to be true, I couldn't keep on keeping on...through my own heartache...and through our ministry which exposes us to so many who are burdened with incredibly heavy and overwhelming heartaches.

Teaching people the Word, showing them where to turn in the midst of their pain and confusion, helping them develop and deepen their relationship with Jesus Christ is what makes the difference.

I cannot change their circumstances; I cannot cure their heartache. I cannot change my own circumstances or cure my own heartache! But I know Who can. And I have learned that despite heartache I can go on and my life can be effective...*and is probably more effective because of it!*

And because I know this on a personal level, I have the same message for others. The cure for your heartache is found in the Great Physician, Jehovah-rapha, and in His healing balm of Gilead, the Word of God.

As a matter of fact, I believe that people who have heartaches and who, in the midst of those heartaches, cling to God and to His Word will be those who are the most greatly used of God to impact their world.

This is the truth with which the Lord encourages us in 2 Corinthians, chapters 1–5. I urge you to take time in the next few hours or days to read and study this passage. Our God is the God of all comfort, and He comforts us so that we may be able with that comfort—that grace, that strength—to comfort others.

> *"Blessed be the God and Father of our Lord Jesus Christ, the Father of mercies and God of all comfort, who comforts us in all our affliction so that we will be able to comfort those who are in any affliction with the comfort with which we ourselves are comforted by God"* *(2 Corinthians 1:3-4).*

Paul tells us that at one point he was so burdened that he despaired even of life, but God comforted and delivered him and used that burden to deepen his trust in God (2 Corinthians 1:8-10).

As He did with Paul, God manifests through us the sweet fragrance of His character, and our heartaches and hurts are the very tools He uses to transform us into the image of His Son.

> *"We all, with unveiled face, beholding as in a mirror the glory of the Lord, are being transformed into the same image from glory to glory, just as from the Lord, the Spirit"* *(2 Corinthians 3:18).*

We are ambassadors for Christ, pointing others away from things which are seen (the temporal) to things which are not seen (the eternal).

So take courage, valiant warrior. Fight the good fight of faith, for soon it will all be over, and then only one thing will matter: "Have I pleased my Father God?"

"For momentary, light affliction is producing for us an eternal weight of glory far beyond all comparison, while we look not at the things which are seen, but at the things which are not seen; for the things which are seen are temporal, but the things which are not seen are eternal" (2 Corinthians 4:17-18).

MY RESPONSE TO HIS WORDS...

My Response to His Words...

When the Forecast Is Bleak

When the weather report says "storms ahead," do you trust God or rent a tent?

It's hard to trust God when it's raining and you want sunshine.

It's hard to trust God for cool but pleasant weather when it is in the mid-90s and in just five days over 1,500 people are going to show up for the outdoor dedication of a new training center...and the extended six-day forecast is for lows in the 70s and highs in the 90s with scattered thundershowers.

It's hard not to rent a tent when that's the weather report. But a tent would cost two or three thousand dollars, and it would ruin the incredible worship service we have planned, with eight-foot banners coming down the aisles bearing the different names and titles of our Lord as the audience worships Him in song.

It's hard, isn't it, to trust God for anything when the "forecast" is contrary to what we want or feel we need.

Maybe it's finances...and the forecast is grim.

Maybe it's a restored relationship...and the forecast is hopeless.

Maybe it's a job...and the forecast is bleak.

Maybe it's a report from the doctor...and the forecast is ominous.

Whatever—and it could be anything—you know that you are totally helpless in the situation. You have done all that you can do, and you still have no guarantee that it will work...that it will turn out "right." So there you stand, wondering if the sun will ever shine and if the breeze will ever drive the clouds away.

What do you do? What can you do?

Well, first you examine your heart to find out if there's any unconfessed sin in your life. If there is, you latch on to 1 John 1:9 and take it, with a penitent spirit, to the throne of grace. There you confess your sins and remember that He promises,

> *"If we confess our sins, He is faithful and righteous to forgive us our sins and to cleanse us from all unrighteousness" (1 John 1:9).*

But then what do you do?

There's only one thing...and it is all that is necessary: You cast all your care on the One who cares for you.

When the apostle Peter wrote his first epistle, he told the hurting, suffering, persecuted Christians scattered throughout Asia Minor to "stand firm" in the grace of God (1 Peter 5:12).

Apparently some of them thought it strange that suffering would come their way, so, among other wonderful things, Peter wrote,

> *"Humble yourselves under the mighty hand of God, that He may exalt you at the proper time, casting all your anxiety on Him, because He cares for you" (1 Peter 5:6-7).*

Roll that burden, that care, that anxiety, that weight off your back and onto His almighty shoulders. You are the sheep of His pasture, and sheep are not burden-bearing animals! He cares for you. *He cares for you.* (Have you got that?!) What concerns you is of the utmost concern to Him.

God has you in His hand, and His hand is a mighty hand. Mighty not only to save and to keep...but mighty to deliver.

He brought the children of Israel "out of Egypt with a mighty hand" when they cried to Him (Deuteronomy 9:26; see also Exodus 2:23-25). Can He not deliver you with His mighty hand?

He cast hailstones on Israel's enemies and made the sun stand still so that "the sun stopped in the middle of the sky, and did not hasten to go down for about a whole day. There was no day like that...when the LORD listened to the voice of a man" (Joshua 10:13-14).

Have you asked God to hear your cry?

Did He not promise to "supply all your needs according to His riches in glory in Christ Jesus" (Philippians 4:19)? Did He not say, "Seek first His kingdom and His righteousness; and all these things will be added to you" (Matthew 6:33)?

God is immutable; He cannot change.

He is absolute veracity; He cannot lie.

He is the same yesterday, today, and forever.

He will not leave you nor forsake you.

Therefore, you can boldly say, "The Lord is my helper, and I will not fear what man shall do unto me" (Hebrews 13:6 KJV).

God's hand is mighty...so mighty that He controls the wind. "He caused the east wind to blow in the heavens and by His power He directed the south wind" (Psalm 78:26). When Samuel called to the Lord, "the LORD sent thunder and rain that day" (1 Samuel 12:18)...and when He wanted, He withheld rain, or sent rain on one city but not another (Amos 4:7).

He is God!

You have done what you can. I have done what I can. Now we must rest in Him. God will do as He pleases, and none will thwart His hand or His will...no matter what "the forecast." God is greater than forecasts. (By the way, it didn't rain on the day of the dedication!)

His throne sits above all the circumstances of life, and

> *"He doeth according to his will in the army of heaven, and among the inhabitants of the earth: and none can stay his hand, or say unto him, What doest thou?"* (Daniel 4:35 KJV).

Cry to Him. If it is for your good and His glory, He will answer. If not, He won't, because what He has planned is better...even though it may rain.

The plans He has for you are plans for good and not for evil, to give you a future and a hope (Jeremiah 29:11).

> *"Who is among you that fears the* LORD, *that obeys the voice of His servant, that walks in darkness and has no light? Let him trust in the name of the* LORD *and rely on his God" (Isaiah 50:10).*

MY RESPONSE TO HIS WORDS...

My Response to His Words...

When You Find It Difficult to Trust God

When you have a need—material, emotional, or spiritual—do you ever feel that you have to do something more than trust, obey, and pray?

We fret. We worry. We strive. We wrangle. We manipulate. We scheme. We're frustrated. We're anxious. We're troubled. We wring our hands in despair. Sometimes we panic.

Why?

Because, Beloved, we do not obey and pray. We do not really believe that God can do what He says He can. We do not really trust Him.

Oh, intellectually we may have it straight that He is sovereign—that He is the ruler over all. But we can't seem to trust His rulership. We may know that He's a God of love. But we forget. Or we resist committing ourselves fully to His care.

Somehow, no matter what we know about God, we don't always feel that we can trust Him. So we try to handle matters ourselves.

Or we forget to consult our Father. We leave Him out of our plans and actions...until we become absolutely desperate.

We forget that God is God...able to change the hearts and minds of men and women...able and willing to supply all of our needs...able to move heaven and earth...able to cause all things to work together for our good and His glory.

Somehow, whatever our need—whether it be material, emotional, or spiritual—we feel that we have to do something more than trust, obey, and pray.

Isn't that true? True, at least, more often than you want it to be or more often than you know that it should be?

Why? Because so often we don't know what it means to commit everything to God in prayer.

I'm not talking about badgering Him in order to get things which are not in His will or in His timing. And I am not talking about trying to manipulate God through your faith—faith in your word or in your "positive confession" rather than in His Word and according to His character.

Rather, I am talking about prayer as a way of life: a constant communion that causes you to commit everything to your Father for His leadership, His anointing, His provision according to His way and according to His time.

True prayer is always according to His will.

Effective prayer, that which is born of the Spirit, does not rip verses out of context, fling them at the feet of God's footstool, and expect Him to answer simply because you have faith. Effective prayer comes when we abide in Him and His words abide in us, and we ask according to His will.

In this age
 when there is so much emphasis on man's abilities,
  on self,
in this age
 when our lives are so busy,
 when we live in the midst of constant noise,
 when "the world" is clamoring for our dollars
 for our allegiance,
 for our attention,

it is so easy to forget to be still and to know that
    He is God,
it is so easy to forget that our Father, who sits as Sovereign over
    all mankind and over the whole world, is waiting for us to
    bring all of our concerns and lay them at His feet.
We forget that He says,

> *"You do not have because you do not ask. You ask and
> do not receive, because you ask with wrong motives, so
> that you may spend it on your pleasures" (James 4:2b-3).*

I have been reading through the Old Testament for my quiet
time, and I don't think I have ever been as aware as I am now of
how sensitive God is to the cries of His people. How often I have
reminded our Father of that lately as I have cried out to Him in my
impotence. And He has not failed me.

Why?

Because He is God, the unchangeable, faithful Father who keeps
His Word.

Just the other day I was reading the story of Hezekiah, one of the
kings of Judah. Let me share a little bit about him, as I believe it will
bless you, as it has me.

Sennacherib, the king of Assyria, had already captured and dis-
persed the Northern Kingdom of Israel. He was on a conquering
rampage. Nation after nation had gone down in defeat to the
mighty Assyrian Empire. Now Sennacherib wanted to add the
Southern Kingdom to his list of victories. He even sent his chief
military officers to the walls of Jerusalem to tell the whole city that
God Himself had told them—the Assyrians—to go up to Jerusalem
and destroy it (2 Kings 18:25).

When this tactic did not cause the people to overthrow Hezekiah
and give up in defeat, the king of Assyria spelled out his plans of
destruction in a letter.

> *"Then Hezekiah took the letter from the hand of the
> messengers and read it, and he went up to the house of
> the LORD and spread it out before the LORD. Hezekiah
> prayed before the LORD and said, 'O LORD, the God of
> Israel, who are enthroned above the cherubim, You are*

*the God, You alone, of all the kingdoms of the earth. You
have made heaven and earth. Incline Your ear, O LORD,
and hear; open Your eyes, O LORD, and see; and listen
to the words of Sennacherib, which he has sent to
reproach the living God. Truly, O LORD, the kings of
Assyria have devastated the nations and their lands and
have cast their gods into the fire, for they were not gods
but the work of men's hands, wood and stone. So they
have destroyed them. Now, O LORD our God, I pray,
deliver us from his hand that all the kingdoms of the
earth may know that You alone, O LORD, are God!'"
(2 Kings 19:14-19).*

If we only looked at the circumstances instead of the One who
is over the circumstances, it would be apparent that Hezekiah had
every human reason to be overwhelmed, even panic-stricken, for the
odds were truly against him.

*"Then Isaiah the son of Amoz sent to Hezekiah saying,
'Thus says the LORD, the God of Israel, "Because you
have prayed to me about Sennacherib king of Assyria,
I have heard you"'" (2 Kings 19:20).*

Do you see it? "...*Because you have prayed...*"

Oh, what would happen if we prayed more?

God's ears are never closed to the cries of His creation.

When we pray—when we consult God, seeking His will, His
guidance, His assistance—we are humbling ourselves. We're
saying, "God, I am not sufficient in and of myself. I am dependent
upon You."

When we don't pray—or when our prayers really amount to
telling God what to do, what we want to have done—we make
ourselves wiser than God by telling Him how to direct the affairs
of a universe that He brought into existence and sustains without
any help from us. We walk in pride, saying, "I can handle life
myself."

To see the lack of prayer as subtle pride throws a new light on
unceasing prayer, doesn't it?

When we built the Grace Kinser Memorial Training Center a
few years ago, the last items to be done were the furnishings. How

we prayed for God's leadership. We wanted everything to be attractive, glorifying to Him, but not extravagant. Decorating a building of that size was something none of us had the expertise for.

So what did God do in answer to our cry?

He sent Judy Henry to Atlanta to look for furniture bargains. While there, she stopped to have Clint Elliott cut her hair. Clint loves the Lord and likes to keep up on the latest happenings at our ministry. As Judy shared her concern about decorating the building, Clint left her abruptly and then called her to the phone to talk to his friend.

As Judy picked up the phone, she could hear the voice on the other end of the line shouting, "Praise the Lord!"

The voice belonged to Ann Platz, a decorator with an outstanding reputation. She'd even decorated the Alabama governor's mansion. Ann was shouting because months earlier after a prayer meeting a friend had approached her and said, "You're going to be asked to do something in Chattanooga. You're to do it." Ann knew no one in Chattanooga, but she kept her ears open for months, waiting to see if this was a true word from the Lord.

It was! And God gave us a decorator par excellence that we could never have afforded—at no charge!

But that's not all. Another shout went up over the phone when Ann learned that she would be working on the Grace Kinser Memorial Training Center, for she and Grace had been good friends. As a matter of fact, Ann bought Grace's condo after Grace went to be with the Lord!

From threats of an enemy to buying material possessions—there is nothing that we should not consult our Father about in prayer.

> *"Be anxious for nothing, but in everything by prayer*
> *and supplication with thanksgiving let your requests be*
> *made known to God" (Philippians 4:6).*

My Response to His Words. . .

When You Must
Stand Against the Tide

What can we do in the battle being fought for the minds and hearts of mankind?

Some time ago I watched a miniseries on television called *The Nightmare Years,* a docudrama centering around William Shirer's years as a newspaper reporter for Hearst and later as a correspondent for CBS.

Assigned to Berlin just as Hitler began making his move to rule Germany, Shirer saw firsthand just how the Führer rose to such total power. Shirer was there through the invasion of Austria, Poland, and France. He stayed until Hitler began threatening England in hopes of getting them to surrender without invasion. When Shirer exposed the fact that Germany was staging an attack against England that they weren't prepared to carry through with, the Gestapo was ordered to kill him. The reporter fled for his life and managed to escape.

Shirer's integrity and sense of responsibility captured my heart. He stayed in Germany at the peril of his life, stood against the Nazi regime, refused to be duped by their propaganda, challenged Hitler's henchmen face-to-face with their lies, constantly called the Reich's hand, and exposed everything he could to the outside world. To me, although he seemingly did not know our Lord, William Shirer was a hero, a role model, an example to many who professed to know our Lord but were swept up in the Nazi deceit.

How did Hitler ever gain the power he did when the man was obviously sick to the core of his being? (That question has always fascinated me.)

He did it by capturing the minds and the hearts of the dissatisfied German people and by focusing on the youth, brainwashing them with lies—lies so indelibly written on their minds that they even turned against their families for the honor and the future of the Reich. Young men and women were turned into hard, insensitive, brutal human beings who beat elderly people on the street because they would not say "Heil Hitler" and who humiliated and brutalized human beings because they were Jews.

Hitler ruled by delusion and by fear. And those who helped him in his reign of horror justified what he did and turned the other way when the man acted like a maniac. Those who worked closest with Hitler chose to believe a lie because if they did not it would cost them their position, their power, or even their lives.

Hitler also deluded the heads of nations, including England, because these leaders wanted peace at any price. They compromised what they believed. They chose to believe a lie rather than the truth, for to believe the truth would have cost them temporal comfort and security. It was easier to look the other way, to deny, or to ignore what they were seeing and hearing; it was easier not to investigate, not to stir things up. They were cowards.

How God spoke to my heart through this account of history! Christianity never removes us from the evil world...it leaves us in it; but we are not to be of that world. We are not to think like the world, act like the world, adapt to the world, or sell out to the world. Instead, we are to contest the world, oppose it, and rescue every soul we can from it!

Jesus never called us to peaceful coexistence and compromise with the world and its temporary prince. Jesus leaves us here to rescue the hearts and minds of men and women and children so that they might know the truth...and in knowing the truth be set free.

Free from the father of lies, the deceiver, the destroyer. Free from the adversary of God and of man—an adversary who lies in wait to deceive, destroy, and take captive the souls of men. Free from the one who tries to blind the hearts and the minds of men and women so that they might not see the glorious light of the gospel of Jesus Christ and be saved. Free from the one who lures them into sin—destructive, enslaving sin where they are held with the cords of their own iniquity.

Just in the one small batch of mail that I worked on yesterday I have letters from two women who are devastated by what they have just found out about their husbands. Yet out of their love for God they are struggling to hold their marriages together...marriages which are being ripped apart because of adultery and perversion that have come because their "Christian" husbands have become ensnared in pornography.

A third letter from a woman determined to stand alone if necessary told of a book which is being used in her child's elementary school. The book teaches children how to make contact with the devil, and the principal won't do anything about it because he doesn't want to make waves!

Like William Shirer, these three women will not buy the lies, they will not compromise, they will not take the road to expediency. But where are the other Shirers today? Where are the people who, like these three women, are willing to seek the truth no matter what the cost? People who are willing to risk their career, their safety, their security, their all for the truth embodied in our Lord Jesus Christ?

Did our Lord call us to have détente with the enemy?

No!

He called us to a cross.

He called us to deny ourselves and follow Him, no matter what the cost.

For His sake and the gospel's, He told us to "be faithful unto death."

There are hundreds...no, make that thousands...of believers in this country and around the world who are convinced and determined that we must capture the hearts and the minds of men, women, teens, and children with the knowledge of God's Word so that they can know how to live—not by the world's standards, but by God's and God's alone.

But that is not all...for it is not enough to live it. God's Word must be propagated; it must be shared and taught. Others must learn how to study His Word for themselves so that they won't be carried about by every wind of doctrine and cunning craftiness of this evil world, which lies in wait to deceive. They need to know truth so that they can use it to set others free. They need to know it so that they can live as salt and light,

> *"children of God above reproach in the midst of a crooked and perverse generation, among whom you appear as lights in the world, holding fast the word of life..." (Philippians 2:15-16).*

When we do, people can see and know that they don't have to be puppets or slaves in Satan's Reich!

Are you constantly aware of the fact that you have been delivered from the domain of darkness? Are you living in the kingdom of light? If not, why not?

Don't be deceived. Be valiant warriors. And, if necessary, be ready and willing to risk your temporal life for Him.

Eternity waits!

> *"We have not ceased to pray for you and to ask that you may be filled with the knowledge of His will in all spiritual wisdom and understanding, so that you will walk in a manner worthy of the Lord, to please Him in all respects, bearing fruit in every good work and increasing in the knowledge of God; strengthened with all power, according to His glorious might, for the attaining of all steadfastness and patience; joyously giving thanks to the Father, who has qualified us to share in the inheritance of the saints in Light.*
>
> *"For He rescued us from the domain of darkness, and transferred us to the kingdom of His beloved Son, in whom we have redemption, the forgiveness of sins" (Colossians 1:9-14).*

MY RESPONSE TO HIS WORDS...

My Response to His Words...

When You Feel Threatened

Are you being threatened with loss?

The loss of a loved one...the loss of position or reputation...the loss of a dream or ambition...if you remain steadfast in your pursuit of the Lord and His Holiness? Are you being challenged because of your commitment to our Lord?

At a time like this, there is only one place to fix your eyes...and it's not on the lions that would devour you!

I've been teaching the book of Daniel, and I cannot tell you what a blessing it has been to my life! It is such a powerful reminder of the incredible accuracy of the Word of God and how we need to be on the alert at all times, for surely the day of His coming is at hand.

And if that's so, things are not going to get easier. More and more we are going to experience the conflict of those final days when the battle lines are drawn and the love of men grows cold...and evil flourishes, increasingly brazen and vile.

However, as we look at the book of Daniel, we see the mighty and all-sufficient power of God displayed in the realm of mankind. We see God in His sovereignty override the plots of evil men and the natural appetites of hungry lions!

I wish you'd stop and read Daniel 6 before you read any further, because I think it will help you better understand what I believe our Father would have me share with you.

Jealous men sought Daniel's demise. But Daniel came out the victor! And those men who had maliciously accused God's servant were themselves devoured by the lions!

Do victories like that just happen? No! Victories like this are won where Daniel's was—on our knees, in our closets, clinging to all that we know of our God.

Convictions are born and holiness is perfected when we are shut up alone with God and His Word in prayer. There in the quiet, set apart from the clamor of the world and its multitude of voices, we hear and learn truth. We get a proper perspective of life…God's perspective.

Then we leave to face the lions, knowing that we may be tossed into their den, but also knowing that they won't devour us. Ultimately victory will come to those who constantly serve Him, to those who won't lay aside their communion with God, to those who don't take their eyes off God.

What do we see in Daniel's life that we need to emulate?

First of all, we see his *commitment.*

> *"They could find no ground of accusation or evidence of corruption, inasmuch as he was faithful, and no negligence or corruption was to be found in him. Then these men said, 'We will not find any ground of accusation against this Daniel unless we find it against him with regard to the law of his God'"* (Daniel 6:4-5).

Oh, how I pray that the commitment of our lives will be as Daniel's, so that even our enemies recognize its strength.

Daniel was also a man of *conviction* and *courage.*

This is evident from his response to the king's decree, which, on penalty of death, forbade everyone from praying to any god or making any kind of a petition to anyone but King Darius. Daniel's heart was so set on obedience to God and so convinced of who He was and of the veracity of His Word that

> *"he continued kneeling on his knees three times a day, praying and giving thanks before his God, as he had been doing previously"* (Daniel 6:10b).

Daniel was also *consistent.*

No starts and stops, no interruptions in his walk. Circumstances could not alter Daniel's relationship with God! And if the powers that be didn't like it, they would just have to feed him to the lions! (Some things are worth dying for if necessary.)

When the king went out to see if Daniel had survived the hungry lions, he called out,

> *"Daniel, servant of the living God, has your God, whom you constantly serve, been able to deliver you from the lions?" (Daniel 6:20).*

Daniel was a man of commitment, conviction, courage, and consistency. His enemies knew it. The king knew it. His God knew it.

And God dealt with Daniel's enemies: The lions that were supposed to devour him ate them instead.

Then God, through Daniel, brought the king to deep conviction. Such conviction that King Darius issued a new decree:

> *"I make a decree that in all the dominion of my kingdom men are to fear and tremble before the God of Daniel; for He is the living God and enduring forever, and His kingdom is one which will not be destroyed, and His dominion will be forever" (Daniel 6:26).*

So when your faith is challenged, when you feel threatened, remember that "by faith" Daniel "shut the mouths of lions," and you can too (Hebrews 11:33).

Your God is a lion tamer!

> *"Therefore, my beloved brethren, be steadfast, immovable, always abounding in the work of the Lord, knowing that your toil is not in vain in the Lord" (1 Corinthians 15:58).*

MY RESPONSE TO HIS WORDS...

My Response to His Words...

When You Feel
You Can't Go On

---

*Do you ever want to turn tail and
run when the going gets tough?*

Are you on the verge of surrendering hope or your convictions because you are weary of waiting...of facing adversity...of enduring trials...of standing up for what is right...of resisting wrong...of walking in obedience to the commandments of God when others think you a fool?

Why is it a struggle for any child of God to go on?

To face life?

To keep on keeping on?

To walk in His commandments when disobedience, unbelief, or at least compromise seem more logical, more convenient, more expedient?

Is it because we think we know better than God?

Is it because we fear the face of man?

Is it because we want to please or at least live in harmony with those around us?

Is it because we fear the future? Worry about the unknown? The unexpected?

Is it because suddenly we think God isn't doing His job—or isn't going to do it? Or that He doesn't care? Or that He's not able?

When the children of Israel were on the verge of entering Canaan to take possession of the land and evict its godless inhabitants, Moses said to them,

> *"Be strong and courageous, do not be afraid or tremble at them, for the* LORD *your God is the one who goes with you. He will not fail you or forsake you"* *(Deuteronomy 31:6).*

Just before Jesus left His disciples to take up Calvary's cross, He told them,

> *"These things I have spoken to you, so that in Me you may have peace. In the world you have tribulation, but take courage; I have overcome the world" (John 16:33).*

Be strong...willing to endure.

Be courageous...facing difficulty or danger with confidence—confidence that God is sovereign and that He will never permit you to suffer more than you can endure...confidence that God will bring His perfect will to pass...confidence that we can trust and obey, no matter how violent the storm, for He is with us.

> *"Take courage, it is I; do not be afraid" (Matthew 14:27).*

Yet, you may be saying: "How can I be strong and courageous when I feel ordinary and unimportant...weak and fearful...disappointed and angry with God?"

Recently I received a letter from one of our Precept students who was in enormous pain. Her godly daughter, whom she adored, had been killed, along with her son-in-law and her grandchildren. In one tragic accident all their lives were suddenly snuffed out.

Now my friend was struggling...wanting to die...fighting anger with God...questioning all that she knows, because God seems cruel.

If you read the Word of God carefully, you know that the child of God is to be strong and courageous—not overcome by circumstances, not embittered with God, not despairing of life, not losing hope. We are always to fight the good fight of faith.

But *how?*

How can this woman—or any child of God—be strong and courageous when we are but flesh? When we feel we cannot go on? When we feel so weak and impotent? When by nature we are "wimps"?

Let me share with you some principles or precepts that will help you be strong and courageous. Take these before the Lord and meditate on them; then ask God how to live in the light of them.

As Joshua prepared to take Moses' place and lead the children of Israel into the Promised Land, God knew the trials and tests of faith that awaited him. Thus, God told him as He tells us,

> *"Just as I have been with Moses, I will be with you; I will not fail you or forsake you....Only be strong and very courageous; be careful to do according to all the law which Moses My servant commanded you; do not turn from it to the right or to the left, so that you may have success wherever you go. This book of the law shall not depart from your mouth, but you shall meditate on it day and night, so that you may be careful to do according to all that is written in it; for then you will make your way prosperous, and then you will have success"* (Joshua 1:5,7-8).

What does it mean to be strong and courageous?

To be strong is not to be weak—weak in trust, weak in conviction, weak in obedience. To be strong is to believe—trusting and obeying, no matter what. And strength is the forerunner of courage. In 1 John 2:14 we read,

> *"I have written to you, fathers, because you know Him who has been from the beginning. I have written to you, young men, because you are strong, and the word of God abides in you, and you have overcome the evil one."*

Note that the young men are strong because God's Word abides in them. And in Deuteronomy 11:8 we read,

> *"You shall therefore keep every commandment which I am commanding you today, so that you may be strong*

and go in and possess the land into which you are about
to cross to possess it."

From this verse it is clear that obedience makes us strong. Isn't that neat?

When we obey, when we believe (obedience and faith are synonymous), strength is ours! In 2 Timothy 2:1 we are told, "Be strong in the grace that is in Christ Jesus." In other words, appropriate what is yours through grace: the unmerited favor and blessing of God which is always at your disposal!

And what about courage? Courage is to be brave. Courage is to have moral strength which enables us to face any danger, trouble, or pain steadily. It is a quality of mind that enables us to meet danger without fear. It is to act as we believe we should.

It's all a matter of acting in faith, for to be courageous you must go forward. You must go on with life, convinced of God's power, God's sovereignty, and God's faithfulness to His Word. You must continue undaunted no matter the obstacles, no matter the emotions. You must not compromise with unbelief, nor can you give up in the face of challenge or adversity.

Obedience makes us strong.

Faith makes us courageous.

My friend who lost her loved ones in that tragic accident—and who's hurting so and being tempted to bitterness—needs to be strong and courageous in all that she knows of God's power, sovereignty, and faithfulness to His Word. She needs to flee into His refuge by laying hold of the hope set before her and all children of God (Hebrews 6:18-20). And I am confident she will.

She needs to remember her heavenly Father is there, arms open wide, promising,

> *"I will never desert you, nor will I ever forsake you"*
> *(Hebrews 13:5b).*

This is how she...you...I...can be strong and courageous and say with confidence,

> *"The* LORD *is my helper, I will not be afraid. What will*
> *man do to me?" (Hebrews 13:6).*

My Response to His Words...

When You Are Gripped by Fear

Are there times when you feel as if an army has come against you?

Maybe they're not all wearing the same uniform, but they all seem to be converging on you at once. As a result, you're having a hard time handling all that life seems to be throwing you at the present.

Nothing definite has been said. But in your heart of hearts you're sure that certain people are not pleased with you. You can tell by the way they act, the way they look at you, their tone of voice, or by the fact that when you appear on the scene they either change the subject they are discussing with others, or they simply walk away.

Your mind is going crazy. You're scared. And fear is doing funny things to your body. Maybe it's not open combat, but you feel the chill of a cold war. You don't know what's going to happen, but you just have a feeling that it's not going to be good. Maybe your stomach is in knots...or maybe you can't sleep.

What do you do?

Well, first of all you need to remember that your

> *"struggle is not against flesh and blood, but against the rulers, against the powers, against the world forces of this darkness, against the spiritual forces of wickedness in the heavenly places" (Ephesians 6:12).*

If you think people are coming against you, there's someone behind it all—the enemy of every child of God, that serpent of old, the devil, the accuser of the brethren, the father of lies. What you're imagining may or may not be fact, but either way it's torment! His fiery darts have started fires that are hard to extinguish.

So what do you do?

You need to remember that the battle is not yours but the Lord's! And because it is His and not yours, it must be fought His way. You are to stand firm in the Lord and in the strength of His might (Ephesians 6:10). Just as God told His people Israel that they would not be delivered by horses or chariots or a multitude of armies, but that their deliverance would come from the Lord! He assured them that He would fight for them! So the Lord is your Covenant Partner! Don't go into battle without the Captain of the Host.

And how do you remember all of this when you fear for your welfare...or when you shudder at the thought of what the future may hold...or when you simply hurt because others have come against you?

You need to do what Jehoshaphat, the king of Judah, did when he heard that a great multitude was coming against him.

> *"Jehoshaphat was afraid and turned his attention to seek the LORD, and proclaimed a fast throughout all Judah" (2 Chronicles 20:3).*

Jehoshaphat knew where to turn. He knew where his help would come from. Listen:

> *"O LORD, the God of our fathers, are You not God in the heavens? And are You not ruler over all the kingdoms of the nations? Power and might are in Your hand so that no one can stand against You. Did You not, O our God,*

drive out the inhabitants of this land before Your people Israel and give it to the descendants of Abraham Your friend forever? They have lived in it, and have built You a sanctuary there for Your name, saying, 'Should evil come upon us, the sword, or judgment, or pestilence, or famine, we will stand before this house and before You (for Your name is in this house) and cry to You in our distress, and You will hear and deliver us'" (2 Chronicles 20:6-9).

And although Jehoshaphat did not know specifically what to do, he knew where to look. He said,

"O our God...we are powerless before this great multitude who are coming against us; nor do we know what to do, but our eyes are on You" (2 Chronicles 20:12).

Do you feel threatened?

Tell God. Cry to Him.

Are you gripped by fear?

That spirit of fear does not come from God. Resist it.

"For God hath not given us the spirit of fear; but of power, and of love, and of a sound mind" (2 Timothy 1:7 KJV).

Listen to Jehoshaphat's proclamation of faith:

"'Do not fear or be dismayed because of this great multitude, for the battle is not yours but God's....You need not fight in this battle; station yourselves, stand and see the salvation of the LORD on your behalf, O Judah and Jerusalem.' Do not fear or be dismayed; tomorrow go out to face them, for the LORD is with you" (2 Chronicles 20:15,17).

Bow your head and worship the Lord. Look at His "worthship." Believe that He is who He says He is, and that He will do what He says He will do.

"Put your trust in the LORD your God and you will be established. Put your trust in His prophets [in the Word]

and succeed....Give thanks to the LORD, *for His lov-*
ingkindness is everlasting" (2 Chronicles 20:20-21).

If you'll follow these steps, you'll find sweet release—sweet victory.

1. Submit to God. Talk aloud to God. Tell Him that He can do
anything He pleases with you. Confirm again your desire to serve
and follow Him fully. Tell Him that your one and foremost passion
is to be found pleasing to Him, that you want Jesus to be exalted
in your body, whether by life or by death (Philippians 1:20).

Now, if your heart's desire isn't to be pleasing to Him, then ask
God to show you why it isn't.

> *"Draw near to God and He will draw near to you.*
> *Cleanse your hands, you sinners; and purify your*
> *hearts, you double-minded. Be miserable and mourn*
> *and weep; let your laughter be turned into mourning*
> *and your joy to gloom. Humble yourselves in the pres-*
> *ence of the Lord, and He will exalt you" (James 4:8-10).*

2. Now, take the authority that is yours as a child of God and command the enemy to be bound on earth as he is bound in heaven
(Matthew 16:19). The gates of hell cannot stand against His church.
You are bone of Jesus' bone, flesh of Jesus' flesh, and "greater is He
who is in you than he who is in the world" (1 John 4:4).

So, stand firm in the Lord and in the strength of His might. Take
the sword of the Spirit, which is the Word of God, from your
sheath and command the enemy to be gone as Jesus did.

And finally, as Jehoshaphat did, go forth singing praises to your
God. The Lord will ambush the enemy. You watch. I have seen the
reality of these truths in action in my own life and in the lives of
others.

It's war! The enemy's time is short! Jesus is coming soon! But thanks
be to God who always causes us to triumph *in Him.* Remember that
true victory is only found in faith's obedience to His Word. As you go
forth to battle, keep bringing every thought captive in Jesus Christ
and don't give the devil any place in your mind or in your life.

> *"Submit therefore to God. Resist the devil and he will*
> *flee from you" (James 4:7).*

My Response to His Words...

When the Future Is Uncertain

Does looking into the future leave you feeling uncertain or apprehensive? How are you going to face it...and make it?

Events over the past few years have been astonishing, haven't they? Our nation attacked. Our troops at war again. More and more upheaval in the Middle East.

In many instances our hope has been stirred. In others, we are discouraged, even fearful.

People by the thousands have lost their jobs. Our government's debt looms threateningly over us, and yet we continue to give away billions of dollars. Taxes claim a major portion of our salaries, yet more and more of our tax dollars are spent to cover the ineptness and graft of men.

Physical calamities suddenly devastate homes. Rage and brutality are tearing apart our cities. AIDS is a major threat to the welfare of our nation, but people still refuse to forsake the sin that is spreading the disease.

The innocent are jeopardized, and the guilty are protected. We call good "evil" and evil "good."

In the midst of all this, we feel impotent to do a thing about all that is happening. It is as though we are caught in a current of swift-moving events that are about to dash us against the jagged rocks of an almost amoral nation. Deep in our heart of hearts we know, don't we, that unless things change radically God is going to have to judge our land?

What do you do in times like these when the future is so uncertain? Let me share some things I believe the Lord has laid on my heart.

Although the future is uncertain to so many, it is not uncertain for believers.

If you read and study the Bible, you can see that the events occurring in Europe, the Middle East, and Israel are valid indicators that our Lord's coming is near. Things are not going to get better...only worse. Therefore, it is imperative that you're prepared and that you have fulfilled your duty in preparing your family.

How?

You need to evaluate your lifestyle. Take inventory.

What is important? What's occupying your time? Where are your priorities?

It is absolutely crucial that you develop a strong and intimate relationship with the Lord. If you know Him and His Word, you'll have a security that will keep you from being shaken in the storms that are on the horizon.

God has given you a multitude of promises to cover every contingency of life, but you cannot appropriate what you don't know...or believe. God said, "According to your faith be it unto you." God doesn't run any "Second-Hand Faith Shops." Your relationship with Him is your number one priority, for it keeps every other relationship in its proper place.

The reason so many marriages and families are falling apart is that we have failed to build a proper relationship with God through His Word.

Also, you must learn God's Word so you won't be led astray. In the last days there is going to be a great deception and a falling away from the faith. You must not be deceived! And in that regard, not knowing the Word of God could be disastrous.

You need to build your relationships with family and friends.

One of the major reasons our society is falling apart is that we have neglected interpersonal relationships. We're too busy—even doing good things.

In the last days the love of many will grow cold toward one another and toward God. God said that.

Many parents lose their children to the occult, to drugs, to alcohol, and to promiscuity because the security of a strong sense of family, love, and discipline is missing. If you have children or grandchildren, you have this responsibility. If you neglect it, Beloved, you'll answer to God.

Turn off the television, and talk to one another. Open your home to others. A television set that portrays perverted, decadent lifestyles will be little comfort, help, or companionship in the days to come. It will give you its version of what's going on, but it won't hold your hand or meet your needs in the trials.

Invest in the work of God.

Your treasures here are going to be destroyed, so put your money in the Lord's work, which will pay eternal dividends. Watch how you spend your money. Concentrate on the necessities rather than the luxuries.

I know that may not be as much fun right now, but it will keep you from being ashamed when you see Him face-to-face and when you have to give an account for your earthly stewardship. And when you do invest your resources, make sure those to whom you give are accountable.

Let's seek to know our Father better, strive to live a more godly life, and live as an overcomer through these last days.

> *"Set your mind on the things above, not on the things that are on earth"* (Colossians 3:2).

My Response to His Words. . .

When All You See Is Devastation

---

*Does it seem like the world
is falling apart?*

You are not the first person to feel this way.

As the prophet Amos sat down to write the prophecies God had given him, his first words were,

> *"The LORD roars from Zion, and from Jerusalem He utters His voice" (Amos 1:2).*

The days of Amos were like our days; and his message is to become ours:

> *"A lion has roared! Who will not fear? The Lord GOD has spoken! Who can but prophesy?" (Amos 3:8).*

In all the events taking place in the world today, the Lion is roaring, the Lord is speaking, and if you know the Word of God, the message is very clear:

> *"Prepare to meet your God" (Amos 4:12).*

These five words have been ringing in my heart. They are pealing from the bell tower of heaven—alerting us to the near coming of the Lord, calling us to repentance and prayer, warning us to prepare for the days ahead because the day of the Lord is close at hand.

The Bible tells us that what was written beforehand in the Old Testament was written for our learning and admonition so that through perseverance and encouragement we might have hope (1 Corinthians 10:11; Romans 15:4). It was the prophets of old who told us of the days and events which would usher in that dread and terrible day of the Lord, for

> "*surely the Lord* GOD *does nothing unless He reveals His secret counsel to His servants the prophets*" *(Amos 3:7).*

As in the days of Amos, God is trying to get our attention through His divine judgments—the earthquakes, the floods, the fires, the economy, the wars and rumors of war around the world,

> "*Yet you have not returned to Me*" *(Amos 4:6).*

The prophet Amos sounds for us a call to repentance, to prayer—a cry from the throne of God through His prophet:

> "*Seek Me that you may live....Seek the* LORD *that you may live, or He will break forth like a fire...and it will consume with none to quench it....Let justice roll down like waters and righteousness like an ever-flowing stream....Seek good and not evil, that you may live; and thus may the* LORD *God of hosts be with you....Behold I am about to put a plumb line in the midst of My people*" *(Amos 5:4,6,24,14; 7:8).*

As God brought His judgments of locusts and fires out of control upon Israel, Amos interceded, and the Word tells us,

> "*The* LORD *changed His mind about this*" *(Amos 7:6).*

It is not too late! Earnest prayer uttered from repentant hearts vindicates God's justice when He, in mercy, spares His people.

Like the nation of Israel, God has given our country special privileges because of our spiritual heritage and because we were, at one time, governed by leaders and a societal worldview permeated by a reverential fear of God. However, special privileges bring specific responsibilities, and when these responsibilities are neglected, we incur a greater judgment.

Look at what has happened to nations who turned their back on the light God gave them. Take heed! If Israel, the chosen nation of God, was not exempt from the judgment of God, neither shall we be! God's divine and just judgment can only be averted by returning to the obedience of righteousness.

What can you do?

You must make sure you are right with God.

Ask Him to cleanse your heart so you can lift up holy hands to Him in prayer. The effectual fervent prayer of a righteous man avails much (James 5:16). Pray and keep on praying, but don't stop there.

Call others to repentance and prayer. Gather together, get on your knees, and wait before God. Then beseech Him in prayer as He leads by His Spirit. And keep on meeting until God breaks forth, or until He tells you to stop.

Also, you need to invest your time and your money in activities and ministries which will reap eternal dividends.

God told Amos that a day was coming when there would be a famine in the land for the hearing of the Word of the Lord and people "will go to and fro to seek the word of the LORD, but they will not find it" (Amos 8:12).

As I read these verses, I am reminded of what it is like in China, and in Russia and Romania and other formerly Communist countries where there's been a famine for the Word of God. Now that the doors have opened in some of these countries, all sorts of cults and pseudo-Christian charlatans have moved in. God's people there must learn how to study God's Word themselves so they will have God's plumb line to check out all they hear and are taught.

We must equip people to know God's Word for themselves and thus to know God. As the saying goes, rather than give them fish, we want to teach them how to fish so they can feed themselves. Then, when and if the day comes that there is a famine for the Word of God in our country and elsewhere, there will be a multitude who not only know their God and His Word but are able to stand and do exploits for Him and to give bread and understanding to the famished.

It is the mandate of the church to take those whom God saves and establish them in His Word as that which produces reverence for Him.

Ask God what He would have you do. Then do it.

"Prepare to meet your God" *(Amos 4:12).*

My Response to His Words...

When Your Expectations Aren't in Him

When it's all over, what is really going to matter?

Not that I've pleased you, or my husband, or my children. Not that people approve or disapprove of me. Not what I had, what I lacked, what I accomplished, or what I failed to achieve.

All that will matter is whether or not I have pleased my Lord by believing what He says and living accordingly. I am to be one man's servant—the Lord's. I am to live by one book—the Bible.

When our expectations are in anything or in anyone other than in pleasing Him, we will know only distress, defeat, disappointment...and failure (even though in reality we did not fail).

Oh, to say with Paul—and mean it—

> *"To me, to live is Christ, and to die is gain" (Philippians 1:21).*

It mattered not that Paul was in prison, confined there for over three years. It only mattered that the work of his Lord continued...that Christ was preached.

In fact, in the midst of his confinement, Paul's one hope and earnest expectation was that he would be ashamed in nothing, but that with all boldness, as always, Christ would be magnified in his body.

As I write this, I have been having my own time of being "shut up"—physically unable to speak or teach. I have been so weak that I have had to be totally still—alone and quiet—as I recuperate. And it has been wonderful! (Does that sound strange?) Because once again, taking me away from the distractions of life (many of them very good things in themselves), our Lord has given me the opportunity to be still and know that He is God. And in doing so, He has reminded me anew, afresh, that only pleasing Him matters.

During these days that I've been "set aside," I've sat on the porch and enjoyed the spring—reveled in the dogwood and azaleas we planted a few years ago and delighted in the mass of color from tulips planted as a birthday surprise. I've eaten when I wanted to eat, slept when I've wanted to, and I've worked on a new Precept course on 2 Thessalonians (but I haven't pushed). I've rented the movie series on Winston Churchill that I've been wanting to see. I've turned on the stereo and listened to George Beverly Shea sing the wonderful old hymns of the faith and to Dino play music to calm the soul.

I've listened to the Bible on tape, and, of course, I've prayed and read—especially in the Psalms. In doing so, I've noticed the gamut of emotions and situations David had to deal with; and I've seen how, through it all, even in his failure and sin, David never let go of God. And when his life was over, God called David a man after His own heart!

In all this, weak though I've been, often to the place of tears, I've found rest. Rest in the promises of our Father, rest in the assurance that nothing depends upon me. It all depends on Him. I'm simply to trust and obey, to be still and know He is God.

But I couldn't be still, I couldn't rest in the midst of trials, in the pressure of ministry, in the weakness of my flesh, if I didn't know my God and His Word.

So what God has shared with me, I wanted to share with you…just in case you needed it too!

May we make knowing Him and His Word our priority and passion so that in the day of testing we will be able to rest in faith. And, in doing so, we'll please Him, which, above all, is our calling.

> *"Be still, and know that I am God;*
> *I will be exalted among the nations,*
> *I will be exalted in the earth" (Psalm 46:10 NIV).*

My Response to His Words...

When You Are
Unable to Cope

⸻

What are you looking for that you cannot find?

⸻

What do you need? What do you long for? What void is not being filled?

Do you think it can be met by another human being? Do you think that if you only had the right person, the right relationship, things would be different? Someone you could be secure with, someone who wouldn't fail you or abandon you, someone who would understand and always be there for you, someone who could provide for you?

If you do, you will only continue to be needy and unfulfilled.

What you need is Merry Christmas—and Happy New Year! You need the relationship that is what Christmas is all about. You need Jesus, God in the flesh, the only One who can give you access to the Father. A Father who not only promises to supply all your needs through Jesus Christ, His Son, but One who is capable and willing to do so.

> *"My God will supply all your needs according to His riches in glory in Christ Jesus" (Philippians 4:19).*

But where does the "Happy New Year" come in, you might ask. Why do I follow "Merry Christmas" with "Happy New Year"?

Because that is what it can be for you if you will believe and embrace this truth in the fullest sense. Your year can and will be different. Your outlook on life can and will be radically transformed.

Oh, your circumstances may not change, the human relationships you so long to alter might remain the same, but it will be a new year for you. Why? Because you will no longer be looking to another human being to meet your needs; you will be looking to God. And God never, ever fails. He cannot fail because He is God.

He is always there. He always has the answers. Nothing can ever drive Him away. No one can ever drive Him away.

Your personality, your behavior, your response will never alter who He is or what He has promised. He is God; He cannot change.

Have you stopped to consider that everything you are going through right now—every void, every unfulfilled longing—has been permitted by a sovereign God in order to draw you to the one and only wellspring that can intimately satisfy you?

It's to draw you to God's Christmas tree—the cross—where He hung His gift—His only begotten Son—for you. The tree where God not only displays and proves His love and commitment to you, but where you find life in death. Life through your death to all else and everyone else but Him is found at the cross.

If you are a child of God and have been miserable, dissatisfied, or unable to cope, it is because you have left the cross.

Life is there—at the cross. Nowhere else.

Peace is there—at the cross. Nowhere else.

Purpose is there—at the cross, where you find your reason for living.

If you have been miserable, dissatisfied, unable to cope, it's because you have walked away in disbelief. If you ever want your deepest needs met, you can't walk away! If you ever want to fill that void within, you can't walk away!

> "He who loves his life loses it, and he who hates his life in this world will keep it to life eternal. If anyone serves Me, he must follow Me; and where I am, there

*My servant will be also; if anyone serves Me, the Father
will honor him" (John 12:25-26).*

If your happiness is wrapped up in pleasing God—in doing His
will, in serving His purposes—then no person, except you, can take
your happiness away. Jesus will be your joy, and the joy of the Lord
will be your strength (Nehemiah 8:10).

Go get a stone—a big enough stone to write on. Then, with a per-
manent marking pen, write EBENEZER on it and say with Samuel:
"Thus far the LORD has helped us" (1 Samuel 7:12). Ebenezer
means "the stone of help."

Put the stone in a prominent place where you'll see it every day.
Then, when you look at it, remember God's cornerstone, the foun-
dation stone that He laid in Zion almost 2,000 years ago.
Remember His words:

> *"Behold, I lay in Zion a choice stone, a precious corner
> stone, and he who believes in Him will not be disap-
> pointed" (1 Peter 2:6).*

MY RESPONSE TO HIS WORDS...

My Response to His Words...

When You Are Offered a Crown Without the Cross

Who are you following?

It's prime time for America—and for Christianity. Prime time to take a good look at ourselves. At who we're following, at where we're going, at what we value.

When *PrimeTime Live* aired its investigative report on three televangelists, I was sick, as I am sure you were if you saw the program. When I saw how funds are solicited and how the responses of faithful listeners and supporters are handled, my heart was grieved. Madison Avenue techniques and manipulative schemes are being used to raise money for the "ministry" of God.

As I watched, I thought, *Father, why do they give to ministries like this? Why are they "hooked" by the appeal?*

People often give because in some way someone touched their heartstrings, which motivated their giving.

Sometimes people give in order to get: They buy "the premium" and think they are in turn helping a good cause. Both the giver and the receiver benefit.

Others give out of a sense of what I might term "religious superstition." They think that if a certain person prays, God will hear. Or they believe that if prayer is offered from a special place, the prayer is more effective. Tied in with this mind-set is a twisted thinking that for one reason or another a donation must accompany the prayer request. So people send their prayer request to that "certain person" along with their donation.

Some people think that if an "empowered" person lays his hand on the outline of their hand where they've written their request, then it will come to pass.

Why do they think the person is empowered? Usually because the speaker claims a special anointing or because they've done something to supposedly demonstrate that power, such as healing a person or reading a letter which affirms their power. Or a prophecy or a word of knowledge is given, and a viewer or listener calls in to confirm it. Therefore, it's assumed that the speaker has certain powers which put him a cut above ordinary Christians.

What's the problem with all this?

The problem is that this person is elevated above the average believer and then, in a sense, takes on the role of a mediator.

Oh, how this breaks my heart, for there is One, only "one mediator...between God and men, the man Christ Jesus" (1 Timothy 2:5).

When the apostle John fell at the angel's feet, even the angel said, "Do not do that; I am a fellow servant of yours and your brethren who hold the testimony of Jesus; worship God. For the testimony of Jesus is the spirit of prophecy" (Revelation 19:10).

It is *prime time* for Christians in America to quit putting people on pedestals! We are all fellow believers, just parts of the body of Christ. Not one of us is sufficient alone. Nor is any part of the body to be exalted—except the head. And Jesus is the head (Ephesians 1:22).

Let's love one another, but let's not exalt anyone but Jesus. After all, as I keep telling our people, "Any old bush will do to be set on fire with the fire of God."

It's *prime time* for us to remember that

> *"there were not many wise according to the flesh, not many mighty, not many noble; but God has chosen the foolish things of the world to shame the wise, and God*

> has chosen the weak things of the world to shame the things which are strong, and the base things of the world and the despised God has chosen, the things that are not, so that He may nullify the things that are, so that no man may boast before God. But by His doing you are in Christ Jesus, who became to us wisdom from God, and righteousness and sanctification, and redemption, so that, just as it is written, 'Let him who boasts, boast in the LORD'" (1 Corinthians 1:26-31).

People also give because they like a person's or a ministry's doctrinal stand. It sets well with them. It goes with what they believe or what they want to believe—or with what they hope is true.

Some give because they have confidence in the ministry, trust the leadership, and feel called of God to have partnership in what the ministry is doing.

Sometimes people give out of a sense of guilt or duty. The appeal implies that if you don't take a certain action, then you haven't done your part for the "cause." For instance, you may be asked to sign a petition, but you are also told to enclose a check with it so that your petition can be delivered by the sender along with others. Have you ever thought how much more effective it would be if every individual sent his or her petition directly to the person or group being petitioned? It would carry far more weight to get thousands of personally addressed envelopes than a stack of petitions in one pile.

It's prime time for Christians to examine why they give and if their giving is pleasing to God.

It's prime time for Christians to be led by the Spirit instead of Madison Avenue.

It's prime time for Christians to start thinking and praying instead of allowing themselves to be manipulated.

Who are we going to follow?

And where are we going?

There's so much to be done, and time is so short. We must not waste God's money.

We have a world to reach with the Word of God. We cannot squander our resources, for we will be held accountable for the stewardship of our finances—for what we give and for what we spend.

I'll never forget when a certain Christian organization and their recreational facilities were going under. People still kept sending them money. They literally poured it down a drain. And what were they valuing? A place to vacation!

Where, oh where, is the cross! It's prime time we remember that when Jesus called us, He made it clear that if we wish to come after Him, we must deny ourselves, take up our cross, and follow Him (Mark 8:34-38).

The cross is for now. The crown comes when Jesus returns. No cross, no crown.

We need to remember Jesus' last words in Revelation:

> "Behold, I am coming quickly, and My reward is with Me, to render to every man according to what he has done" (Revelation 22:12).

I am grieved when I think of the valuable work that many ministries are doing...when I think of how the gifts of God's people could be used in so many places in the world where it would really count and meet vital needs.

I am grieved by the reasons that motivate some people to give, and I am grieved by who and what they give to.

And I am grieved for those who give their money, their family treasures, and their trust to those who would lead them astray!

My heart breaks for those people because they are like sheep without a shepherd, and they've been devoured by wolves in sheep's clothing. Shepherds who have sheared the sheep and used their wool for themselves (Ezekiel 34:1-19).

It's prime time to serve our Lord.

Pray that you'll continue to look to our precious Lord in all things—and pray this for the whole body of Christ.

Pray that you will realize and discern the times and be about His business while it's yet day...while there's still time—and pray this for the whole body of Christ.

And pray that you'll know and be established in the Word of God—and pray this for the whole body of Christ. For...

"we are no longer to be children, tossed here and there by waves and carried about by every wind of doctrine, by the trickery of men, by craftiness in deceitful scheming; but speaking the truth in love, we are to grow up in all aspects into Him who is the head, even Christ, from whom the whole body, being fitted and held together by that which every joint supplies, according to the proper working of each individual part, causes the growth of the body for the building up of itself in love" *(Ephesians 4:14-16).*

My Response to His Words...

When You Don't Know Where to Run

What difference does it make if I'm not in the Word of God on a daily basis?

So you don't know the Bible well, but you're not a preacher or a teacher.

What difference does it make?

You read the Word of God a little. You're here and there in the Bible, but you don't get much out of it.

What difference does it make?

It makes a critical difference. And I can tell you, from my own experience as well as the experience of others, that once you're in the Word consistently, once you've learned how to dig out its treasures of truth for yourself, you will experience the incredible, revolutionary difference.

It's the difference between a "Hi! How are You? By the way, I've been meaning to tell You..." relationship with God and a deep intimacy with your heavenly Father.

It's the difference between a panic attack in the unexpected jolts of life and a supernatural peace in the midst of the worst storm.

It's the difference between confusion and quiet confidence.

It's the difference between a dogmatic, hard-nosed, and sometimes belligerent stance and moving in a gentle and patient, but uncompromising, way.

It's the difference between a restless, I-don't-know-what's-missing-but-something-is kind of feeling and a surety that all is well with your soul.

It's the difference between running off in a thousand different directions and a knowing that this is what you are to do.

Spending time with God in His Word—knowing Him, His ways, and understanding what He has said—gives you a sense of stability.

Those who know God through His Word and through daily intimacy with Him retain the healthy fear (respect and trust) of Him that God says we are to have. Yet at the same time, that unhealthy dread of what God might do if they submit to Him disappears, for they know His character and comprehend the depth of His love. And perfect love casts out fear because fear has torment (1 John 4:18 KJV).

When you know Him and His Word, you know where to run for refuge, you know where to rest your case, you know who has all the facts. And this knowledge eases all the tension as you enter the rest of faith.

When you spend time daily with God in His Word, your faith grows, for faith comes by hearing, and hearing by the Word of God (Romans 10:17).

Anyone who wants to know God's Word intimately can! Children, teens, and adults!

Those who do begin their personal study of the Bible on a daily basis and live by what God says will soon discover that being in the Word is like gathering manna every day. It is food for life.

> *"He humbled you and let you be hungry, and fed you with manna which you did not know, nor did your fathers know, that He might make you understand that man does not live by bread alone, but man lives by everything that proceeds out of the mouth of the LORD"* (Deuteronomy 8:3).

They will discover the sufficiency, the all-sufficiency of the Word of God.

We say that we believe the Bible is the Word of God. We say that we believe it is without error and contradiction, thus, holding to its inerrancy. But do we hold to its sufficiency?

If we say something is sufficient, we mean it is adequate; you need nothing in addition to it!

Do we realize that the solution to every problem, every hurt, every dilemma can be found between the covers of His holy Word—in its precepts, principles, examples, commands, promises, warnings, and teachings?

- Do we partake of it daily so we can be nourished and made strong, prepared for every situation of life?

- Do we dwell on its precepts and wrestle with how they are to be lived out in our relationships, in our businesses, in our social lives?

- Do we run to its pages and to its Author for wisdom (counsel) when we don't know what to do, where to turn, or how we are going to survive?

- Do we bring our questions, our frustrations to God's inerrant Word?

- Do we give Him the time to speak to us?

- Do we wait, as Habakkuk did, to see what the Lord will speak to us so that we might walk by faith (Habakkuk 2:1-4)?

Or do we run to the arm of flesh, the counsel of men, the latest theories and philosophies?

Do we seek out the popular counselors, speakers, and writers of our day, listening to their philosophies, evaluating their successes, and then seeing if we want to apply it to our situation?

Or do we first wait upon the Lord and then stay or go at *His* direction?

The Bible says, "The fear of the LORD is the beginning of knowledge" (Proverbs 1:7a).

The word for "fear" means a reverential trust and awesome respect. If we really respect God for who He is, then we will make listening to Him a priority. If we fear Him, we'll trust what He says and live accordingly, no matter what the situation. Then we'll have His wisdom for every situation of life.

Let me share with you something Charles Stanley said in his book *A Touch of Wisdom:*

> *The Scriptures are God's wisdom. They teach us who God is and reveal how He acts and thinks. They instruct us to distinguish right from wrong, and they give clear guidelines for practical living. His Word is counsel from heaven for life on earth, revealing the Father's omniscient heart to help us walk victoriously in all our endeavors.*
>
> *When learned and consistently applied, God's Word fastens firmly together the disjointed portions of our lives—our work, our family, our relationships, our dreams, our thoughts, our words, our deeds—in the sturdy framework of divine wisdom.*
>
> *This is the foundation on which to build a life that can courageously withstand the inevitable storms of criticism, pain, loss, temptation, and success.*

There is no other foundation, Beloved! No other is needed, because the Word of God is totally sufficient.

If you, like Habakkuk, will embrace the Word of God and bring every dilemma and lay it at the feet of God's Word, then you'll find yourself walking with hinds' feet and not slipping.

> *"So faith comes from hearing, and hearing by the word of Christ"* (Romans 10:17).

MY RESPONSE TO HIS WORDS...

My Response to His Words...

When You Get Weary Following the Lord

Have you discovered that following Jesus is not easy?

In fact, do you sometimes wonder if you really made the right decision?

Are you weary of waiting, of trusting? Do you wonder why God doesn't act immediately...why He doesn't do something right now?

Do you feel that if you don't take things into your own hands and do it your own way, you really may get more messed up?

Sometimes do you even wonder if He really cares? If He's even there at all? Or maybe all this "faith business" is a figment of people's imagination! Or—and you may be hesitant to verbalize it—a hoax?

Jesus never indicated that following Him would be easy.

Throughout His ministry, He reminded His followers that there was a cost and that they needed to count it. Of course, there were promises of heavenly rewards—someday no sorrow, no pain, no tears. *But,* those rewards were for the future, not for today.

Today would not be without temptation, trials, testings, difficulties, and challenges. In this world they would have tribulation.

Of course, with that statement He did promise them peace—in Him (John 16:33).

At first many followed Him simply because of the miracles, the free lunches of loaves and fish.

However, as they listened closely, they heard that there was more to following Jesus than seeing miraculous things happen and eating free meals. Following Him meant identification with Him—and Jesus' popularity was waning. His sayings had become difficult.

And "as a result of this many of His disciples withdrew and were not walking with Him anymore."

As the many walked away, Jesus said to the twelve disciples, "You do not want to go away also, do you?"

And what was their answer?

"Lord," Simon Peter said, "to whom shall we go? You have words of eternal life" (John 6:66-68).

Yes, He does have words of eternal life. They're not words of death, but of life. They're not just for today, but for eternity.

He knows our past, our present, our future. He's been there, and He will be there for all of our present and future circumstances.

His words are truth—not lies, like the enemy's. They're the daily bread which nourishes our soul so we can confront and manage each day and all that He allows that day to bring.

All of us face times of incredible warfare in our lives—often on a multitude of fronts. Where do we turn?

The only place to turn is to the One who has words of eternal life!

He is still on the throne. Neither His character nor His promises have changed. We must simply cling to Him as the waistband clings to the waist (Jeremiah 13:11).

We must walk by faith. There is no other way to walk. All we have to do is make sure we are righteous in our ways "for the steps of a good man are ordered by the Lord" (Psalm 37:23 KJV).

I don't know specifically where you are, what is going on in your life, what you are dealing with or facing, but I do know that He has the words of eternal life for you. If you will believe Him, if you will spend time in these "words," if you will study them, hide them in your heart, and determine that you will live by them, then you can know you will walk as more than a conqueror.

However, you know what our problem is, don't you? Many times the last place we run is to the Lord and to His Word. Or because we have not disciplined ourselves and given the Word of God the priority it requires, then we don't have the answers, the wisdom, the guidance, the comfort, the promises, the direction that the Word gives us.

The psalmist put it well:

> *"If Your law had not been my delight, then I would have perished in my affliction. I will never forget Your precepts, for by them You have revived me. I am Yours, save me; for I have sought Your precepts"* (Psalm 119:92-94).

His words are different than all the words that have ever been or ever will be recorded any other place in the world.

Jesus said,

> *"The words that I have spoken to you are spirit and are life"* (John 6:63).

This is why we've devoted our lives to getting every individual we can into His Word. For we know that in knowing the Word and knowing Him through the Word, they can be at peace even in the storm. They can quit struggling in their circumstances and snuggle into the security of His sovereign, unconditional love.

It works! It works!

I wish you could read the mail we receive as person after person writes to tell us what has happened since they started studying God's Word inductively.

One precious woman wrote to tell of God's sufficiency in her recent tragedy. She was riding on a tractor with her husband, cutting down some small trees, when a branch from another tree knocked him from the tractor and threw him under the bush hog. She frantically tried to stop the tractor. By the time she was able to stop it, the bush hog was on top of her husband. She wrote...

As I stood there, I couldn't believe what I was seeing. My husband had on laced-up work boots, jeans, and a flannel shirt, and everything he had on was torn completely off him. But, Kay, as I stood there, I felt God's hands picking me up and His arms around me, holding me ever so gently. People say I went into shock and if that is what they want to think, that is fine with me because I know what I felt and God Himself promised me in His Word that He will never put anything on me that I cannot bear. My husband was gone, but God is not a liar. He has kept His promise. I have a peace inside that I cannot explain.

No, life is not easy. Following Jesus doesn't mean we are exempt from trials or tragedy. But it does mean that we have someplace to go—because He has words of eternal life.

Are His words familiar friends to you? Are you spending time in them each day, feeding on them?

"These things I have spoken to you, so that in Me you may have peace. In the world you have tribulation, but take courage; I have overcome the world" (John 16:33).

MY RESPONSE TO HIS WORDS...

My Response to His Words...

When You Are Confronted by Giants

What do you do when suddenly confronted with an insurmountable situation?

What do you do when suddenly you're confronted with something you never expected and it doesn't look good? The situation looms like a giant, and you can't help but tremble. Fear pierces your heart. Your eyes dart from one face to another looking for some glimmer of hope, some confirmation that things are not as critical as they seem. But what you see only confirms the darkness of the hour.

What do you do? How do you keep from falling apart? How do you face this giant of an impossibility when in your own eyes you are about as powerful as a grasshopper?

You have three options: You can decide there is no way out and run; you can be carried along by what you see, what you hear, what you're experiencing, and your own impotence to change things; or you can run to the promises of God and cling to them in sheer faith.

The latter option is always there. As a matter of fact, it is the only option that carries a warranty with it. Yet it is often hard to choose this option because you cannot see the reality, the substance of its guarantee. Deciding upon this option is strictly an act of faith!

When we face this type of situation...when life takes a totally unexpected turn...one we are not prepared for...we have to make a choice.

The best choice? Choose by faith to walk by what we know about God, what we've studied in His Word, and what we've proclaimed with our mouth.

These times of testing are not unlike the one the children of Israel faced when they received the report of the ten spies who had just returned from scouting the land of promise.

Hopes were high when the twelve spies left for the Negev. They were going in to spy out a land that God had promised them, a land which would be their home forever. Their slavery in Egypt had come to an end—no more mud pits. Their journey would soon be over, their dreams realized.

Then the twelve returned.

Yes, they said, it was a land flowing with milk and honey just as God had promised. Why, they had even brought back a cluster of grapes hanging from a pole to prove it.

But...but there were giants in the land!

Giants? They had never expected giants!

To ten of the twelve spies this spelled defeat. When the people looked at the faces of the ten, they could see the fear.

So what if the other two spies, Joshua and Caleb, were not abashed by the situation?

So what if they reassured the people that God was still in control, still able to give them the land despite the giants? Who should the people believe—the ten or the two? The ten who looked at the situation and sized it up realistically—or the two who were trying to persuade them to believe God regardless of what they saw with their own eyes?

What did they do? You remember.

The children of Israel grumbled against God.

Moses and Aaron, however, fell on their faces before God.

When we are threatened and confronted by giants we haven't even dreamed of, like the children of Israel we have a choice. We can look one of three directions.

- We can look at the giants and say "no way" and continue in the wilderness of unbelief.

- We can look at our own impotence to change the situation and, as a result, never go for the promised land.

- Or we can cling to the promises of God, trusting that although everything might not come out according to our plan, according to our evaluation of the situation, or on our timetable, it will work out together for good as He promises. We can choose to believe the promise that His will, His Word, His work will not be thwarted by any giant or any situation of man (Isaiah 14:24-27; Daniel 11:32b).

When we meet giants, we can say, as Caleb said, "If the LORD is pleased with us, then He will...." We can fall on our faces before God, as Moses and Aaron did—not in retreat or defeat, but in submission to His will. We will do our part and leave the consequences to our sovereign God.

The sky may be absolutely black; the wind may be howling; we may be wondering if we will ever get home...yet we can rest in Him. God never leaves His throne.

Let's not leave the place of our appointment. Let's stay on our faces before His throne, knowing that whatever God wills, He can bring to pass. No matter the giants, His Word remains true. Our responsibility is to know it and to believe it.

I don't know what kind of giant is looming before you, Beloved, what disappointment you have to face, but I can tell you with utmost confidence that God is no respecter of persons, only a respecter of faith.

Don't give up! Don't run back to Egypt (the world) for help! Don't wander in the wilderness!

Trust God's intentions and His capabilities.

> *"Commit your way to the LORD,*
> *Trust also in Him, and He will do it" (Psalm 37:5).*

My Response to His Words...

When You Feel
Far Away from God

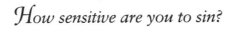

How sensitive are you to sin?

What would you do if I told you that judgment was coming? Would you tell me that you didn't want to hear about it? Or would you say that you don't care whether judgment comes or not? Or would you say that you don't believe it?

Please give me a few minutes to talk with you about this, for it may bring about the awakening of a deepened relationship with your heavenly Father...a newfound freedom...a revival in your own life.

Let me begin by going back to one of the Old Testament prophets.

Balaam was a prophet of God. He was also the prophet whom Balak, the king of Moab, wanted to hire to curse the children of Israel so that he could defeat them. Balaam was also the one whose donkey talked to him because he wouldn't listen to God!

But because God had blessed the children of Israel, Balaam was unable to curse them. However, Balaam got around that by counseling the daughters of Moab to "play the harlot" with the men of

Israel. So they invited the Israelites "to the sacrifices of their gods, and the people [the Israelites] ate and bowed down to their gods" (Numbers 25:2; read the whole story in Numbers 22–25).

This angered the Lord.

> *"The LORD said to Moses, 'Take all the leaders of the people and execute them in broad daylight before the LORD, so that the fierce anger of the LORD may turn away from Israel'"* (Numbers 25:4).

God was telling His people that what was happening had to come to a halt or His fierce anger would be poured out on Israel! They were the ones responsible to execute judgment immediately, and if they did not, God Himself would move in judgment.

In the midst of all their licentiousness and their idolatrous carryings-on,

> *"one of the sons of Israel came and brought to his relatives a Midianite woman, in the sight of Moses and in the sight of all the congregation of the sons of Israel, while they were weeping at the doorway of the tent of meeting. When Phinehas...saw it, he arose from the midst of the congregation and took a spear in his hand, and he went after the man of Israel into the tent and pierced both of them through, the man of Israel and the woman, through the body. So the plague on the sons of Israel was checked. Those who died by the plague were 24,000"* (Numbers 25:6-9).

What checked this awful plague that was wiping out the children of Israel? Listen to the Word of the Lord:

> *"Phinehas...has turned away My wrath from the sons of Israel in that he was jealous with My jealousy among them, so that I did not destroy the sons of Israel in My jealousy"* (Numbers 25:11).

God's wrath—His judgment—was turned away because sin was properly dealt with!

Oh, how often we neglect this side of God's character! We love to hear about His love and eagerly clutch it to our heart, but the fact that God is righteous, holy, and a God of wrath is a reality that we either deny or want to ignore.

If, as the Word says, the things which were written beforehand were written for our learning and admonition, is there not a great lesson for us in this account?

Isn't God angry at our sin? Isn't He grieved over the adulterous hearts of His people who tolerate sin in their midst, closing their eyes to it in their own lives or churches...or who laugh at sin, enjoy it, and are entertained by it?

Sin must be purged or dealt with. And that's where judgment comes in. Either we judge ourselves...or God judges us! Whichever happens, after judgment there is either revival or the hardening of hearts.

Many maintain that revival is coming—not judgment. However, I believe, along with others, that the revival which will come to America will not come in the stadiums but in the catacombs. And you'll remember that the catacombs were where the Christians hid during the awful time of Roman persecution.

Guide, a homosexual magazine published in Seattle, Washington, in November 1987 laid out a strategic plan for gaining support for the homosexual community. First and foremost was "desensitization of the American public...to help it view homosexuality with indifference instead of with keen emotion."

In the years since, we can see how their plan has been succeeding. Their strategy is the same strategy the devil has used on the church of Jesus Christ—desensitization of Christians in respect to sin.

The purity of the church of Jesus Christ is the only hope for our country. When we are pure, then we will take away the world's cloak of excuses for their sins. And when we are pure and holy, then we are not under the judgment of God. Only then are we able to be used as instruments of righteousness, holding forth the word of life in the midst of a crooked and perverse generation.

How sensitive are you to sin...

- in your own life?
- in the life of the church?

- in your community?
- in your nation?

Has sin—even the slightest of sins—driven a wedge between you and God, between you and your loved ones?

Do you feel far away from God—or even slightly distanced from Him?

If you find yourself feeling numb to the things of God…if you feel your fervor for God cooling even slightly, carefully examine your thinking and reasoning—your inner man—and carefully examine your activities—your outer man—to see if you have allowed sin to cohabit in your heart.

God does not want sin in your life. He is still a jealous God; *Qana* (Hebrew for "jealous") is His name (Exodus 34:14).

Guard your heart! Immorality, wickedness, greed, and spiritual seduction are going to increase. And those who do not guard their hearts will fall prey to these things.

You can talk the talk and even to a degree walk the walk, so that the outward man seems to be right with God—but God doesn't look on the outward as man does…God looks on the heart.

He knows what's within, and He says,

> *"Watch [guard] over your heart with all diligence, for from it flow the springs of life"* (Proverbs 4:23).

But you cannot guard your heart if you do not take time to be alone with God…if you do not wash your heart and soul with the Word of God…if you do not commune with your heavenly Father in prayer.

It is the pure in heart who will see God.

God has made every provision you need, as His child, to keep your heart pure. However, it is your responsibility to appropriate His provisions and live accordingly.

No excuse will be accepted when you stand before Him!

Remain pure. Guard your heart so that you are steadfast, immovable, always abounding in the work of the Lord, so that you won't fall into the snare of the enemy who desires to sift you as wheat.

There's no need to fear Satan if you'll fear God by guarding your heart. Watch what enters your mind. Watch your desires. Bring every emotion to Him, and if it's not in accord with His Word, reject it—and you'll keep your heart pure.

Oh, Beloved, don't put this off. The enemy would seek to distract you, to make you forget to do it, for he knows that it is unrecognized, unconfessed, unforsaken sin that gives him a stronghold in your life.

It is our holy, immutable God who tells us in His Word that

> *"if we judged ourselves rightly, we would not be judged.*
> *But when we are judged, we are disciplined by the Lord*
> *so that we will not be condemned along with the*
> *world" (1 Corinthians 11:31-32).*

My Response to His Words...

Words of
GRACE

When You've Failed

When you've failed, do you wonder how things can ever be the same between you and God? Do you wonder how you can pick up the pieces and begin again?

Thoughts race through your mind: *Can God ever use me again?...Does He even want me?...Will things ever be the same with us?*

You may think you have destroyed your opportunity for a meaningful and joyous life. You may feel doomed to live forever in the shack of your failure—barely surviving—rather than ever again experiencing joy, satisfaction, peace, and fulfillment.

Do thoughts such as these visit you, engaging you in conversations of "what might have been...if only"?

Are you frightened by the knowledge that God is in control—wondering how He will deal with you?

Do you want to run but don't know where to run?

Or do you know that the person, the thing, the object, the situation to which you would run would only displease Him more?

Does despair offer to cover you in its own blanket of hopelessness?

Do you want to hide from life's consequences, cowering in the corner of inertia?

Don't you know that you belong to the God of all grace?

Grace is the birthright of every child of God. Grace is there to preserve you in the darkest night of your failures. His grace—sufficient for all your sin, for all your failure, for all your inadequacy, for all your powerlessness—is yours to claim.

Grace calls you to get up, to throw off your blanket of hopelessness, and to move on through life in faith. And what grace calls you to, grace provides.

Grace is unmerited favor bestowed on us at the moment of our salvation. The kingdom of heaven is reserved for those who become as little children, for those who look to their Father in loving confidence for every benefit, whether it be for the pardon so freely given or for the strength to do His will,

> *"for by grace you have been saved through faith; and that not of yourselves, it is the gift of God" (Ephesians 2:8).*

How often we fail to understand this! We fail to appropriate His grace, which is there to cover our failure and to save us from despair. Instead, we seek to live in our own strength and to approach God on our own merit rather than on His grace.

Yet if it took grace to save us, how can we think that it takes our own skill to make it in the Christian life? Since our own effort and merit couldn't take care of our sin and failure in the first place, what makes us think our own efforts or merit can reinstate us in God's favor?

We will never cease to need our Father—His wisdom, direction, help, and support. We will never outgrow Him. We will always need His grace. The apostle Paul learned this lesson well, as he said,

> *"He has said to me, 'My grace is sufficient for you, for power is perfected in weakness.' Most gladly, therefore,*

I will rather boast about my weaknesses, so that the
power of Christ may dwell in me" (2 Corinthians 12:9).

What amazes me is that some people can be secure enough in the
grace of God to die, but not to live.

I thought about this as I read a note a woman had handed to me
during one of my seminars at the Gaither Praise Gathering. Written
on lined notebook paper and folded many times, the story gripped
me.

Several months earlier this woman, in despair over a sin she had
committed—a sin she had thought she would never commit—took
an overdose. God had graciously spared her life, but now she was
ready to try again. The pills were in her purse, the letters to her husband and four children were written. Everything was set. Death
was better than life. She wouldn't have to face anyone anymore
except God, and surely He would understand—life was just too
much to bear.

But during my seminar God had spoken to her. Hope had
revived.

> *I am going to get rid of the pills, which will be a big*
> *step for me, because I know I can't get any more lethal*
> *pills because of my [first] attempt. Holding onto them*
> *has been a way out. Thank you for being open and*
> *sharing yourself and God. Please pray for emotional*
> *healing from memories that bind me to the past.*

As I finished reading the note, I tried to find out who had handed
it to me. I asked Martha, my secretary, and Evelyn, my assistant,
who had been with me and were running the book table, if they
remembered who had handed me the note. None of us knew!

My heart sank, and I closed my eyes, trying to remember. I had
to get to this woman! We started to pray.

Peace came...and joy. I knew that if I needed to talk with her,
God would bring her back. After all, during the seminar she
attended He had led me to say something that I had been surprised
to hear myself saying: "You may be sitting here listening to all this
and be planning to go home and kill yourself. You may have your
letters written and know exactly how you're going to do it and

when." I had not planned to make that statement; it was not in my notes or in my mind until the moment the Lord prompted me to say it...and thus spoke very specifically to this woman's heart.

The Lord has often done things like this during my years of teaching. And yet it never ceases to thrill my heart or to cause me to stand in awe at our God and His sovereign ways.

However, I couldn't help the direction of my thoughts. It was the last day of the Praise Gathering. How would I find her among the maze of faces? Would she have the boldness to come back to our booth and identify herself? Or would she linger around the table, expecting me to remember her and respond to her note? And if she came and I didn't recognize her, would she again feel rejected?

"Oh, help, Lord!"

And help He did...because He's a God of grace. The woman and her friend came by the table, and her friend let me know she was there. In the midst of that crowd, with arms reaching across the table to get to the books and tapes, questions being asked, money being counted out, checks written, books autographed, and hugs given, at last I was asking her if she had gotten rid of the pills.

"Honey, you need to give them to me. I'll get rid of them."

"But they're my security blanket," she said as she looked over her shoulder.

"Did you mean what you wrote me in your note? Are you really going to be obedient to God, to trust Him?"

"Just a minute—" and with that she was gone. Her friend followed, stopped her, and then she was gone again.

"She'll be right back," her friend said. "She saw her husband and wants to wait until he's gone."

No sooner was the explanation given than the woman was back, pressing a pill bottle into my hand. I slipped it into the pocket next to her note, hugged her, and told her to write.

She was gone as suddenly as she had appeared. But I had the pills!

At midnight, as we were packing up the books, a doctor who had attended one of my seminars came by to talk. Remembering the pills in my pocket, I took them out and showed them to him.

"Do you know what these are? Could they kill a person?"

He knew. There were enough there to kill more than one person, he said.

I walked across the hall to the ladies' room, pushed open the enameled door to the stall, opened the bottle, turned it upside down and watched the dark beige pills hit the water and dissolve. I lifted my foot, pressed the handle, flushed the toilet, and knew that God's grace was sufficient not only for death, but for life.

Oh, my friend, have you learned that lesson yourself?

We believe God will save us.

But so often we forget that the same grace that saves us is the grace that keeps us, enabling us to survive day in and day out, no matter what.

There's always grace to begin anew. There's always grace to keep you. Don't let His grace be poured out on you in vain. Say with Paul,

> *"Not that I have already obtained it or have already become perfect, but I press on so that I may lay hold of that for which also I was laid hold of by Christ Jesus. Brethren, I do not regard myself as having laid hold of it yet; but one thing I do: forgetting what lies behind and reaching forward to what lies ahead, I press on toward the goal for the prize of the upward call of God in Christ Jesus" (Philippians 3:12-14).*

My Response to His Words...

When You Must Forgive

*How important is it to give and to
receive forgiveness?*

A few years ago I received a letter from a woman whose twenty-year-old handicapped son had been murdered. The letter was short and terse. She was hurting beyond belief, and she was justifiably angry at what had been done to her beloved son.

Suddenly life was empty, she said, and the pain was almost unbearable. His death was so senseless, so cruel. Another young man and his girlfriend, high on marijuana, Valium, and alcohol, decided that they wanted her son's car, so they murdered him.

Where was God? she cried. *Why did this happen? How can I go on?*

I wrote back and sent her my booklet *The Sovereignty of God* along with the prayer that the God of all comfort would reach her through His truths.

About a year later she wrote again, telling me that my letter and the booklet had been "so helpful and precious." As a memorial to her son, who in his own life had known so much about hurts, the woman also had purchased a set of our *Lord, Heal My Hurts* tapes for her church and had been part of a group that got together to do the study.

All went well, she said, until they came to the lesson on forgiveness!

Until then, she thought she had it pretty well together. She had even prayed for the salvation of her son's murderers. But she did not dream that God would require her to forgive them!

After all, she reasoned, the Bible says we are to forgive "our brother." These two were not her "brothers"; they were ungodly sinners. To forgive a white lie was one thing; to forgive murder—the murder of her beloved son—was quite another.

As she said this to the group, another woman agreed with her, telling her how the Mafia had killed her younger brother when he was only sixteen.

Then another woman, very young in the Lord, timidly spoke up and said, "But Jesus forgave those who killed Him." They learned that when she was nine months pregnant, this woman's first husband had beaten her so severely that he not only killed the baby she was carrying, but injured her so that she would never be able to have a child. "It took me ten years," the woman said, "but when I finally forgave him, I was set free."

The other two women listened, but were still not convinced that they had to forgive.

Then they listened to my teaching tape, "and," the first woman wrote, "the wonderful Holy Spirit told me, 'You know your son has already forgiven these people. You can do nothing less, and you must let them know your feelings.' So at that moment I truly forgave them, knowing it was what Jesus and my son wanted me to do. I had to leave immediately after the lecture, so I bent over and told the young woman whose sixteen-year-old brother had been murdered what had happened. She said, 'The Holy Spirit told me the same thing.' So both of us were set free that day."

Following this, she said, she wrote to the young man who had murdered her son, enclosing a copy of her son's funeral bulletin and a tape of the funeral service. She told him she did not send this to hurt him, but at the end of the service her pastor had given everyone the opportunity to hear the gospel message and to ask Jesus into their heart, and she wanted her son's killer to hear that.

About a month later the woman received a letter from the mother of the man who had murdered her son.

> *Our son called us yesterday after receiving your letter.*
> *He couldn't believe that you could and had really for-*
> *given him...We cannot thank you enough for your*
> *courageous letter. By it, once again, I have been shown*
> *the loving power of God. He always makes good out of*
> *everything, even something this tragic. I wanted so*
> *often to write you and express our grief that such a*
> *thing happened, but I couldn't seem to find the words*
> *to express our sympathy and sorrow at your loss. Your*
> *letter was the thing that let me know I could write*
> *without giving you more grief.*
>
> *Today I know how the love of God through Jesus*
> *Christ can work in all our lives and allow us to love and*
> *forgive. I'm so grateful for your letter and truly believe*
> *it will be the turning point in our son's life to change him*
> *into the man we've hoped and prayed for him to*
> *become for a long time.*

Forgiveness! How we all need it.

God came into the world in the form of man to reconcile us to Himself (Hebrews 2:9,14). But there could be no reconciliation until His Son, who knew no sin, was made sin for us (2 Corinthians 5:21).

The manger was shadowed with a cross! Jesus was born to die so that you and I, who in no way deserve it, might have forgiveness of sins. Jesus died that we might live!

Our sins were the nails that held Jesus on Calvary's tree. His innocent and untainted blood seeping from His head, His hands, His feet, and His side was the propitiation for our sins. For without the shedding of blood, there is no remission of sins. And we were justified—the guilty declared righteous—because even on that cross Jesus did the will of the Father, saying,

> *"Father, forgive them; for they do not know what they*
> *are doing" (Luke 23:34).*

Jesus—the only One who had a right to condemn—forgave.

And if He is willing to forgive us when it was our sins that caused His death, and if God the Father is willing to forgive, can we, who have so grievously sinned against Him, withhold forgiveness?

Listen to our Savior's words:

> *"Pray, then, in this way....Forgive us our debts, as we also have forgiven our debtors....For if you forgive men for their transgressions, your heavenly Father will also forgive you. But if you do not forgive men, then your Father will not forgive your transgressions"* *(Matthew 6:9,12,14-15).*

That's about as plain as you can get: God will not forgive us if we do not forgive others.

The kingdom of God is made up of men, women, and children who have sinned against God and yet have been forgiven—whatever the depth or extent of their sin.

In all the history of mankind, there is only one man who has never sinned and, therefore, needs no forgiveness. That man is our Lord Jesus Christ. And even totally innocent as He was, He forgave.

What right then do we, as forgiven people, have to withhold forgiveness from others?

Is there anyone you are not willing to forgive? Read Matthew 18:21-35 very carefully.

Are you hurting because you have sinned and cannot believe that God will forgive you? Jesus, the Lamb of God, was born to take away your sins—past, present, and future. There is no other sacrifice for your sins, so stop trying to make one. There is no other atonement, so stop trying to cover your sins. There is no other pardon, so receive it. He says,

> *"If we confess our sins, He is faithful and righteous to forgive us our sins and to cleanse us from all unrighteousness"* *(1 John 1:9).*

Accept His forgiveness and give it.

> *"Be kind to one another, tender-hearted, forgiving each other, just as God in Christ also has forgiven you"* *(Ephesians 4:32).*

My Response to His Words...

When Intimacy with God Seems Impossible

How can I make it across the lake to the shore of Christlikeness? I'm barely staying afloat!

Ever feel that way? Like you're treading water and about to go under?

God says, "You shall be holy, for I am holy" (1 Peter 1:16), and you wonder, "How, O Lord, how?" Being holy seems incomprehensible to you when you look at your own sins and frailties.

I understand how you feel. I've been there. But let me share something I read this morning which ministered to my own heart:

> *If you hear a teaching and feel as though it were unattainable in your condition, you have only heard half the message. You missed the grace which is always resident in the heart of God's truth.*
>
> *Truth without grace is only half-true. Remember this always: Grace and truth are realized in Jesus Christ (John 1:17). What God's truth demands, His grace will provide.*

> *Our minds must be fixed upon grace, otherwise we*
> *will always be overwhelmed and withdrawn from the*
> *Presence of God.* *

If you are going to be holy, the first thing you must realize is that God's grace is not only available but that it is sufficient enough to make it happen.

What God demands, grace provides.

But how? That is the question.

Well, if you are going to be holy, you are going to have to develop an intimate relationship with your Father God. Being holy means having a life of intimacy with God and a life of power (which is what God calls us to).

God says,

> *"You will seek Me and find Me when you search for*
> *Me with all your heart. I will be found by you"* *(Jeremiah*
> *29:13-14).*

Seeking God—intimacy with God—must be your priority.

Maybe knowing God intimately has not been a priority...or maybe you're so overwhelmed by simply trying to meet the demands of daily living that you don't see how knowing God intimately at this stage in life could be a priority. That may be why you feel like you're treading water.

You're not alone!

Many Christians are dealing with the same thing. It's called the tyranny of the urgent. And here's where God's children must walk by faith.

Seeking God doesn't mean that you are to stop earning your living, but it does mean that you may have to be satisfied with less, rather than working harder and longer hours in order to have more!

Seeking God may mean you will have to lay aside some of your time-consuming activities. Television, sports, hobbies, more money, more education, extracurricular things may have to go—and maybe some of your ambitions. But not your work. God says that if you don't work, you shouldn't eat. Besides, He promises that if

---

* Francis Frangipane, *Holiness, Truth and the Presence of God* (Marion, Iowa: Advancing Church Publications, 1986), pp. 23, 27.

you seek His kingdom and His righteousness, the basics of life (food and covering) will be provided (Matthew 6:33).

Of course you'll never see the fulfillment of this promise until you do what God says. But when you begin seeking Him, God in His grace will move on your behalf. And He will allow you to find Him, for He cannot lie. God keeps His promises!

And how do you seek Him?

You begin by being in His word consistently...day in and day out. Three minutes a day isn't going to do it! Give God a minimum amount of time—say an hour. It's less than a tithe of the 24 hours that make up a calendar day. Remember that God said that you are to search for Him with all your heart. Is an hour too much to give?

Diligently digging into the Word of God will take the "ho hum" out of your relationship with Him.

As I write that statement, I think of some of our brothers and sisters in Moldova (formerly Moldavia in the Soviet Union) who have told us that their Christianity has taken on new joy because now they are studying God's Word. After long hours of daily labor, their one pursuit is studying God's Word.

These dear people who don't even have enough soap to bathe told us, "We are richer than Abraham and Melchizedek because we have this Precept Bible study to help us in knowing God and His Word."

Their priorities are straight. They have discovered where their true riches lie—not in the abundance of material possessions, but in knowing God intimately and in knowing the power of His Word.

What about you? I know life in these United States offers a multitude of distractions. But don't let them rob you of intimacy with God. Don't let them rob you of the power of God in your life. Don't let them rob you of *holiness*.

Don't swap what is temporal for that which pays eternal dividends. If you do, you are a fool. Satan, the prince of this world, has deceived you.

Intimacy with God and holiness come when you make God your priority, when you get into His Word...*and* when you spend time with Him, praying and waiting on Him to speak to you. Waiting until in the inner man you know He is saying, "This is the way, walk in it."

It is there—waiting before Him in prayer—that you will gain great confidence in God and in His will for you each day of your life. Because your goal is not simply to know His Word, but to know the God of the Word intimately, you cannot neglect prayer.

Don't you want to know Him so intimately that your heart touches His, until your hearts beat as one? Then you must learn to do more than pray, "bless...bless...bless...give me...help me." You must be still enough to hear His voice. Prayer is searching for the heart of God.

And once you find it, you will know that your sins are covered and your frailties do not matter. In prayer, through His grace, your impotence is filled with His power.

God is looking for men, women, teens, and children who will tremble at His Word—for those who do will seek to be holy even as He is holy.

"I love those who love me; and those who diligently
seek me will find me" (Proverbs 8:17).

MY RESPONSE TO HIS WORDS...

My Response to His Words...

When Troubles and Disappointments Come

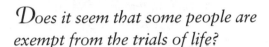

Does it seem that some people are exempt from the trials of life?

I know life can be very traumatic—or if not traumatic, at least disillusioning and disappointing—can't it? And sometimes, when you look at the visible surface of others' lives, it seems that everyone is exempt from trouble and discouragement...everyone, that is, except you.

I don't think anyone is exempt, although sometimes it seems that way.

In times past I've had to deal with envy as I've looked at the lives of others and wished that mine could be like theirs. Then the Lord has graciously given me a glimpse backstage, and I've found out that we all have our problems in one form or another.

I remember at one point telling our kids that I had come to the conclusion that I was an idealist. They all laughed! It had been so obvious to them! Idealists have their dream worlds; they want everything perfect. This is one, among many, of my weaknesses.

The question is, "How can we survive the traumas, the disillusionments, the disappointments—and our own frailties—and live strong and effective lives which will impact the kingdom of God?"

Or, to look at it another way, we might ask, "Why is it that some people remain strong through their weaknesses and difficulties and others don't?"

How can we survive and remain strong in our Lord and in the strength of His might—no matter what comes into our lives?

I believe the answer is found, first, in understanding who you are in Christ Jesus. Second, you need to be absolutely confident of God's unconditional, unchanging love toward you.

As I've observed others over the years, I've seen that when people really believe what God says about them, and when they see themselves as God sees them, they can handle anything that life brings their way, and they are eager to serve the Lord.

However, when you don't understand and embrace in faith what God says about you, you'll find you lack confidence in God—in His unconditional love, in His help, in His promises, and in His desire to use you. Your attention turns to what's wrong in you...to circumstances in your past or in your present situation. That's where your focus stays—and it's the pits.

Instead, your focus should be "on Christ" and on your position "in Christ."

If I could draw a valentine for you, it would be Jesus Christ in the shape of a heart with a picture of you inside the heart.

"In Christ" is a key phrase in the New Testament epistles.

However, it may be that as you read the New Testament the enemy blinds you to this truth and whispers in your ear, "You're a sinner. You're no good. You'll never amount to much. You're certainly of no value to God! You're not good enough, smart enough, or talented enough for God to use you. Look at all that's happened to you—look at where you've been. Look at how you've failed. Remember, you never succeeded in the past—look at your past. You don't have what it takes. Someone else would be better—more suitable, more qualified."

The devil is having a heyday among Christians today because, through one means or another, he's blinding them to who they are in Christ. Satan is feeding them a lie, and they're swallowing the bait—hook, line, and sinker.

And what they have swallowed is ripping out their insides. Has it happened to you, Beloved...in any measure?

This frustration and pain can end if you'll believe God and cling to what He says. Remember that God cannot lie, and He says that if you are His child...

- You are no longer a sinner. You are a saint (one set apart for God). You have received forgiveness for all your sins—past, present, and future (Hebrews 10:10,14-18; Romans 8:1).

- You are no longer bound to your past or to what you were. You are a brand-new creature in Christ Jesus. The old you died, and you have been made brand-new; you are able to walk in newness of life (Galatians 2:20; 2 Corinthians 5:17; Romans 6:4-7).

- You are no longer a slave to sin. As a servant of righteousness, you don't have to let sin rule in your body (John 8:34-36; Romans 6).

- You are no longer part of the kingdom of darkness, but have been seated in heavenly places above all the power of the evil one and his demonic forces (Colossians 1:13; Ephesians 1:19-23; 2:4-6).

- You are no longer rejected but are accepted in the Beloved—just as you are—because God chose you for Himself before the foundation of the world. You have been adopted as God's dear child and are sealed by His Spirit, who guarantees you will live with God forever (Ephesians 1:3-14).

- You no longer have to fear the consequences of your past, for your sovereign God promises that He will cause everything in your life to work together for your good and Christlikeness (Romans 8:28-30).

- You no longer have to fear being rejected, abandoned, left alone, or left without help. God has promised never to leave you or forsake you so that

you can boldly say that He is your Helper; therefore, you need not fear what man will do to you
(Hebrews 13:5-6).

- You no longer have to fear death, for you cannot
  die before your time. Jesus holds the keys to hell and
  death. If and when you die, you will be immediately
  absent from the body and present with the Lord
  (Revelation 1:18; 2 Corinthians 5:8-9).

- You no longer need to fear approaching God. You
  can come boldly to His throne and find His mercy—
  unearned favor and help—in the time of your need
  (Hebrews 4:16).

- You no longer are to fear not having exactly what
  you need. God promises to supply all of your needs
  through Christ Jesus your Lord (1 Corinthians 3:21-
  23; Matthew 6:33; Philippians 4:19).

Take these *truths* and pray them aloud to God each day for the
next month—not mechanically but wholeheartedly.

Thank God for each truth. Then, in faith, tell Him you want to
think and act accordingly.

Read the New Testament epistles, beginning with Romans. Ask
God to show you other truths about who you are in Christ Jesus and
about what is yours because you belong to Him. Begin a list of these
truths, recording all you learn as you read aloud each day.

If you'll do this, you'll find life taking on a whole new dimension.

All of this and more is true because God loved you—just the
way you were—and gave His Son for you. In love, He put *you in*
Jesus Christ and Jesus Christ *in you.*

What more can God do? What more can He say? He's done it
all in His Son. He's said it all in His Word. Now, you must do your
part: Believe!

> "There is now no condemnation for those who are in
> Christ Jesus. For the law of the Spirit of life in Christ
> Jesus has set you free from the law of sin and of death"
> (Romans 8:1-2).

My Response to His Words. . .

When Hope Is Gone

*Has hope become
a stranger in your life?*

Do you look about you…within you…and hurt?

Do you hurt because what you wanted in life has become an impossible dream?

Is your hope gone because it's too late to make your dream come true? The mold is cast, you're poured into it, and the clay is hardened.

Maybe hope is gone because a phase of your life is over, never to be relived, only replayed. And every time it's replayed, your hopelessness increases.

Maybe hope is gone because you're an adult now, and someone or something robbed you of your childhood and youth. You want to be a child again, to have another chance, another start. But it's impossible. So you feel robbed. You look about you at other people, and envy consumes you.

Maybe your hope is gone because you've discovered children pack up and leave home but never move out of your heart. And sometimes you wish they would. Your pain is enormous. Your hopes and your dreams for them are seemingly shattered. Your relationship is cracked and fragile. You wish they were little again so you could do it differently, but there's no hope; the die has been cast. They'll never be children again.

Maybe your hope is gone because the doctor has given his diagnosis, and it spells death. You're not ready to face death emotionally, and even financially you wonder how you will be able to afford to die.

Maybe your hope is gone because the one you loved is gone. The sun still shines; the flowers still bloom; the stars still sparkle; people still laugh—but when you reach over to take your loved one's hand so you can share with the one who would understand, he is not there. And you hurt. And you have to go on, and all the hoping in the world won't bring the person back.

Maybe your hope is gone because all you worked for, all you attained, all you saved for, planned for, and found joy in is gone. And you feel ashamed. If only you had known, if only you hadn't done what you did, maybe things would have been different. Hope is replaced by "if onlys"—frustrating, heart-wrenching, self-accusing "if onlys."

Maybe you have lost hope because you're trapped in a vicious cycle of earning a living, caring for your family, trying to survive, and wondering if this is all there is to life. You're busy—maybe even seemingly successful in the eyes of others—but they don't know what's going on inside. They don't know the pain, the hopelessness. You feel trapped. You're caught in a whirlpool of life and responsibilities you can't escape. And you know you're going to drown without ever knowing whether you could have made it if you had chosen another profession, another time, another place, another way to live.

Without hope? *Yes...* and *no.* Let me explain.

Life will never be painless. When the Bible talks about hope, it never has to do with the "threescore and ten" years we may or may not live. It never has to do with life being the way we want it to be. It never has to do with the fulfillment of our desires. It never contains a promise of bliss to those who believe.

Sometimes we want Jesus Christ just for this life—for our own happiness: for the achievement of our goals...as the solver of our problems...the supplier of our needs...the healer of our diseases...the provider of our necessities...the remover of our problems.

We want Him to be liberator but not Lord. Savior but not successor to the throne. Guarantor but not guardian.

We want Jesus for this life—for the pursuit of our happiness, our fulfillment, our hope of a better life right now.

But "if we have hoped in Christ in this life only, we are of all men most to be pitied" (1 Corinthians 15:19). Jesus is not just for this life. When we live as if He is, we will be most miserable. Miserable and unable to find the deep, abiding peace we so desperately long for—peace that can weather any storm, peace that brings hope.

And where does one find this peace?

At the cross—no place else.

Peace is found only in Christ—Christ crucified and resurrected. Christ triumphant over every pain, every sin, every failure, every disappointment, every heartbreak, every tragedy, every hope for this life. Christ...the Prince of Peace.

Hope, peace, and strength to go on are only found at the cross—*His cross and yours.*

First they are found at His cross, where you have received absolute and total forgiveness for all your sins—past, present, and future.

If you have no peace because of your sins, no hope because of what you did yesterday and beyond, if you think you cannot go on—there is only one place you can change all that, and it's at the cross of Jesus Christ.

Start reading the New Testament and don't stop until you finish. As you read, mark every reference to the cross of Jesus Christ and write down what you learn from God's Word. As you write, ask yourself if you are going to believe God or not. Are you going to walk by what your heart feels, what your mind thinks, what your body craves, what others say? Or are you going to believe God?

It's that simple—and that hard. Simple, in that believing is all you have to do; hard, in that you have to make a choice to believe and not let go no matter what. Simple. Hard. But not impossible!

Either you believe what God did at Calvary and what He said and promised to those who would believe and receive His Son, or you don't. If you believe, you will have hope—hope that has to do with the end result of these "threescore and ten" years, realizing that life doesn't end at death. It begins! Seventy years is nothing in the light of eternity, yet we live as if it's everything.

Which brings us to the second cross I mentioned: yours (and mine).

When Jesus calls us to Himself for salvation, He calls us to a cross—ours. He calls us to "death"—death to self in any and every shape and form.

> *"And He was saying to them all, 'If anyone wishes to come after Me, he must deny himself, and take up his cross daily and follow Me'" (Luke 9:23).*

If you will purposely deny self and take up your cross and keep on following Him, then there is always hope—hope for the crucified. Because at the cross you and I look beyond the pain and disappointment and circumstances to the end result: the joy that is set before us...the promise that *all* things "work together for good to those who love God, to those who are called according to His purpose. For those whom He foreknew, He also predestined to become conformed to the image of His Son" (Romans 8:28-29).

And only the cross—first His, then ours—can conform us into His image.

Oh, Beloved, embrace the cross, for then your hope in Christ will move beyond this present life, and you will be of all men...of all women...most envied; for your hope will no longer be in this life, but in His life—His life in you, His life through you, and your life with Him forever. Then you will walk as more than a conqueror, and you will know a peace which passes all understanding.

There is hope at the cross. Weeping endures for a night—so weep, but know that joy does come in the morning. Spring follows winter. He promised.

> *"And he who does not take his cross and follow after Me is not worthy of Me" (Matthew 10:38).*

MY RESPONSE TO HIS WORDS...

My Response to His Words...

When You Wonder If People Can Tell You Are His

Is your life an expression of the truth that Jesus Christ is worthy of honor, of glory, of blessing?

Does your life demonstrate His worthiness?

"Worthy, worthy is the Lamb."

Someday, Beloved, those words will be our song as we join others from every tribe and tongue and people and nation before the throne of God.

When the Lion of the tribe of Judah, the Lamb of God, takes the seven-sealed scroll from the hand of the Father, we will hear the prostrated elders and living creatures proclaim with a loud voice that He alone is worthy to take the scroll and break the seals.

He is the Overcomer! The One who redeemed us with His blood so that we might reign with Him upon the earth.

With a loud voice, all will proclaim,

> *"Worthy is the Lamb that was slain to receive power and riches and wisdom and might and honor and glory and blessing"* (Revelation 5:12).

Why does God give us this dramatic, graphic glimpse into the future—a scene that is almost beyond our human comprehension? Why does He tell us this now?

One reason, I believe, is so that you and I will recognize and live in the expression of this truth now. So we may live in a way which testifies that He is worthy to receive power and riches and wisdom and might and honor and glory and blessing now in the everyday affairs of our lives.

What the angelic host proclaim in a loud voice—without shame, without hesitancy—should merely be the echo of the way we live our lives. Our lives should be a continuous expression of this one singular truth: "Worthy is the lamb." Worthy, worthy, worthy....

As I see the word "worthy" repeated over and over in Revelation 4 and 5, my mind races back to Ephesians, where, after enumerating the blessings which are ours because we are in Christ and Christ in us, Paul "entreats" us

> *"to walk in a manner worthy of the calling with which*
> *you have been called" (Ephesians 4:1).*

Thus I must ask myself a vital question—and so must you, my friend.

How does my life express the worthiness of the One...

- who conquered sin and death by redeeming me with His own blood?

- who brought me from impotence to power, from abject poverty of spirit to a heavenly inheritance, from man's wisdom to God's?

- who brought me from the state of being without might to a point of strength where I can stand against the varied pressures of natural man, to the point of courage and might where I can stand alone, if necessary, for His truth?

How does my life demonstrate His worthiness?

How is my life an expression of the imprint of the truth that above all else, above all others—including myself—Jesus Christ is worthy of honor, of glory, of blessing?

As we examine our lives in the light of His worthiness, we need to ask ourselves some very practical questions. (Read them aloud.)

- Do the things to which I give myself demonstrate that my Lord is worthy of all power? Does the way I use my abilities, my energies show His pre-eminence in my life?

- And what about my riches—the earthly goods and treasures the Lord has given me? It does not matter how great or small they are. Does my stewardship of these riches demonstrate His worthiness?

- Is the wisdom that I absorb and proclaim worthy of my Lord? Does it honor who He is? Do I always hold to the veracity and sufficiency of His Word in all things? Am I willing to earnestly contend for the faith which was once for all delivered to the children of God (Jude 3), or am I cowardly? I cannot shrink back and still count Jesus worthy of might.

Might can be translated "strength," and over and over, throughout the pages of Scripture, we are exhorted to be strong and courageous. And we can be because of "whose" we are.

It has always interested me that the "cowardly" are among those who will find their part in the lake of fire (Revelation 21:8). Have I deemed Jesus worthy of my strength?

Because "honor" and "glory" are so intimately entwined in meaning, it is difficult to separate one from the other. To honor the Lord is to value Him.

To give Him glory is to give a correct opinion, a proper estimate of who He is.

- Does the way I walk—the way I talk, the way I dress, the way I treat others, the way I spend my time, the way I conduct the affairs of my life—demonstrate the worthiness of my Redeemer?

- Does the way I act in each of these areas give a proper estimate of the life purpose of the One who brought me out of the slave market of sin and set me free? The One who delivered me from the kingdom of darkness and brought me into His glorious kingdom of light?

• Do I walk as He walked—in the light of obedience that honors and glorifies the Father, doing always and only those things which please Him (John 5:19,30; 8:28-29; 1 John 2:6)?

• And last, but not least, what do my lips bring forth? Do they properly bless the Lamb of God?

"To bless" is "to speak well of." When I mumble, complain, or disparage my lot in life, am I proclaiming the worthiness or the wisdom of my sovereign Lord—the One who tells me to count it all joy, to give thanks always for all things? The worthiness of the One who promises me that all will work together for my good and His glory, because it will be used to make me more like Him?

Oh, dear one, remember whatever, whatever, whatever...Jesus is worthy to receive power and riches and wisdom and might and honor and glory and blessing, so give it to Him now so that the new song in heaven might be merely a reverberation of your life here on earth.

He is worthy.

> *"The one who says, 'I have come to know Him,' and does not keep His commandments, is a liar, and the truth is not in him; but whoever keeps His word, in him the love of God has truly been perfected. By this we know that we are in Him: the one who says he abides in Him ought himself to walk in the same manner as He walked"* (1 John 2:4-6).

MY RESPONSE TO HIS WORDS...

My Response to His Words...

When Fear Strikes

---

*When you're afraid,
what can you do?*

If you've ever had to deal with fear, you know that just a word...a thought...a noise...an unexpected call or visit can strike panic in your heart.

With that panic, something happens in your body. There's a tension, a fluttering, a sick feeling. You don't want to feel this way, but you can't seem to control your body's response.

And with that response, something happens to your emotions. It's like you're sitting outside, basking in the sun. One minute everything's bright and sunny, and the next moment the warmth is gone. One minute you're toasty warm, and the next minute you're chilled. Wrapping your arms around yourself, you look heavenward, and you understand the change—a black cloud has covered the sun.

"Fear hath torment," says 1 John 4:18 (KJV).

That's the way it is with fear. Joy, peace, security are suddenly obliterated by its chilling cloud.

What do you do when fear strikes? How do you get your body, your emotions, your heart and mind under control? How do you handle the fear without falling apart? If you can't control fear's cause, can you even hope to handle fear's consequences?

The days in which we live are so difficult, so full of uncertainty. How can you be equipped to handle every contingency of life? How can you be spiritually prepared?

What can you do when fear strikes?

First you need to "be still, and know that [He is] God" (Psalm 46:10 KJV).

When fear hits, our first tendency is to react: to run...to call...to take some sort, any sort, of action—even if it's screaming, crying, or getting hysterical. Yet the only action you need to take at that moment is to get still, to stop, to be quiet.

The original Hebrew translated "be still" in Psalm 46 can also be translated "cease striving."

The Christian life is to be, in one respect, a life of rest. We are to rest in who He is, in what He has promised. We are to rest in Jesus.

Remember...the Son is always behind the cloud.

Second, as you get still, remember that over and over in the Word when God tells us to "fear not," in the same breath He also tells us why. He says, "I am the Lord"..."I am with you"..."I am your shield."

Fear not, because your God is I AM. He is everything and anything you'll need. I AM is His memorial-name to all generations—even to ours (Exodus 3:14-15). God is never anything less than He has been in the past, and He never moves from His throne. He is in charge. He knows the cause of your fear, and He is there for you.

Rest—cease striving. Bury your head in His all-sufficient breast. Call upon your El Shaddai, your all-sufficient Father. He says, "Do not be afraid; I am the first and the last" (Revelation 1:17). He's there before the fear comes; He'll not leave you nor forsake you (Hebrews 13:5-6). He's your Helper, and He will be there when it's all over—ever the same.

Third, remember you are of great value to God.

Fear Him alone. Reverence Him. Believe Him. Trust Him. Don't listen to any other voice or suggestions of condemnation. Whatever has come will ultimately be used to make you more like Jesus. So...

*"do not fear those who kill the body but are unable to
kill the soul; but rather fear Him who is able to destroy
both soul and body in hell. Are not two sparrows sold for
a cent? And yet not one of them will fall to the ground
apart from your Father. But the very hairs of your head
are all numbered. So do not fear; you are more valuable
than many sparrows"* (Matthew 10:28-31).

Fourth, when you become still and cease striving, when you
realize He is there for you, that He is all-sufficient, and that you are
precious to Him...seek Him.

When David feared Abimelech, he said,

*"I sought the LORD and He answered me, and deliv-
ered me from all my fears. They looked to Him and
were radiant, and their faces shall never be ashamed.
This poor man cried, and the LORD heard him and
saved him out of all his troubles"* (Psalm 34:4-6).

Ask God what to do and wait to hear His answer.

The Son never ceases to shine.

Fifth, as soon as possible, get into the Word of God. If you don't
know where to turn in the Word and if God doesn't lay any specific passages on your heart, turn to the Psalms. The Psalms are
there for occasions such as these, for in them you will find His consolations.

*"When my anxious thoughts multiply within me, Your
consolations delight my soul"* (Psalm 94:19).

Find refuge in God and His infallible Word. Read until His peace
mounts a guard around your mind, heart, and soul.

Fear not, little sheep. Your Shepherd is there. Someday when
you turn around you'll see that goodness and mercy really were
following you all the days of your life.

*"Do not fear, for I am with you; do not anxiously look
about you, for I am your God, I will strengthen you,
surely I will help you, surely I will uphold you with My
righteous right hand"* (Isaiah 41:10).

MY RESPONSE TO HIS WORDS...

My Response to His Words...

When You Are Worn, Weak from Waiting

Could you do with a little hope?
A little joy?

Hope for a brighter tomorrow? The surety of joy coming in the morning after a night of weeping?

Or better still, do you wish for the quiet and sure confidence of a future that is not the fruit of your todays or yesterdays?

Have years of waiting for these things dragged on and on? Long years, seemingly never-ending years?

Don't faint, precious child of God. Soon in the midst of the darkest of days, maybe even sooner than you think, your Day of Jubilee is coming, for the fullness of your redemption is yet to be experienced!

Your Kinsman-Redeemer, the Lord Jesus Christ, will soon step to the throne of God and take the seven-sealed scroll from the hand of God Almighty (Revelation 5:1-7). I believe that scroll is the title deed to the earth (see Leviticus 25; Jeremiah 32). And although the breaking of those seals will bring great calamity to the sons of disobedience who now inhabit the earth, this event will culminate in your total redemption and vindication.

Every unjust action, word, deed against your Lord and against you, as the Lord's anointed, will be brought into account. And all those who have scorned your Christ and your commitment to Him will acknowledge that God has loved you and will continue to love you for all of eternity (Revelation 3:9). All this is seen for us in "picture form" in the responsibilities of the kinsman-redeemer (a blood relative) as set forth in Leviticus, Numbers, and Ruth. In these books we see the Old Testament shadow of the New Testament reality—a reality described for us in Revelation 5–22.

Let me share three awesome truths about your Kinsman-Redeemer.

First, Leviticus 25 describes the Year of Jubilee. Every fifty years those who had been sold into slavery could return to their families, and those who had lost the land they once owned would have it returned.

If you've ever felt like a slave to someone or something, you can imagine what it would be like to be free from that slavery. Or if you've ever lost your home or property because you couldn't pay a debt, you can imagine the hope this would bring! Your tears would be gone because the mistakes of your yesterdays—with their consequences—would be wiped away forever.

No wonder God called it a Year of Jubilee! The freedom they had lost and the land they had lost were at long last restored!

All this, my friend, was a picture of what is promised you when you receive the Lord Jesus Christ as your Redeemer! And it was recorded so that you might have hope—hope that can hold you through any dark night of your soul (Romans 15:4). Hope that is yours for the believing!

Thus, we have the first truth: Jesus, our Kinsman, redeemed us at Calvary. He "released us from our sins by His blood" (Revelation 1:5). We are no longer slaves to sin. Sin does not have dominion over us. We've been purchased for God by God, and "if the Son makes you free, you will be free indeed" (John 8:36).

Every child of God has victory over the devil and over his darkness because we have a Redeemer, the Lord Jesus Christ. The problem is that many children of God don't know it and, thus, they don't know how to walk in faith's victory. They still live as though their Kinsman-Redeemer had not set them free from slavery to sin. They yield the members of their body as instruments of unrighteousness when they don't have to!

Beloved, your Year of Jubilee came when you believed that the Lord Jesus Christ is God and received Him as your Savior.

But that's not all we have! Our Kinsman-Redeemer not only won our redemption from slavery to sin, but He also guarantees us that we will rule with Him over this world. Satan will no longer hold the position of the "prince of this world."

Jesus, the God-man, the Lion of the tribe of Judah, the Lamb of God, is about to break the seals of the title deed to the earth. He is about to get back what we lost through Adam in the Garden of Eden: dominion over this earth (Genesis 1:26-28). Satan, the prince of this world, and his children of wrath are going to be defeated when Jesus Christ returns to rule as King of kings. We will rule and reign with Him (Revelation 2:26; 3:21; 5:10).

That's why you should stand strong in faith and not faint or lose hope in the day of adversity. There's more to the story of your redemption than just having your sins forgiven. (The book of Revelation gives you the rest of the story, and it's glorious!)

How crucial it is that you know and are secure in these truths for difficult, trying days of testing are on the horizon. Yet whatever happens, we are not to fear! We are to stand united and strong in the Spirit of truth, knowing that our redemption draws nigh.

The earth is the Lord's and the fullness thereof, and our Kinsman-Redeemer will restore to us what Satan stole when he seduced Eve and became the temporary prince of this world. Jubilee! Jubilee!

Finally, our Kinsman-Redeemer has not only won our redemption from slavery to sin and promised that we will reign with Him on the earth, but He is also our blood avenger.

Life is sacred because man was made in God's image. Yet murder pollutes the land.

In ancient Israel, the kinsman-redeemer acted as his deceased relative's blood avenger (Numbers 35:16-34). The death penalty was instituted by God (Genesis 9:5-6).

Satan was the one who plotted the death of Adam and Eve, and, thus, of all mankind. He was a murderer from the beginning and is behind every murder since then (John 8:44). Thus, Jesus will someday put Satan to death in the lake of fire.

You have a righteous and just God who will bring all this about in His perfect timing and way. So don't lose hope when it seems that the wicked go free and Satan moves forward unchecked.

If, because of all the injustice, you are crying, "How long, O Lord, holy and true, will You refrain from judging and avenging our blood on those who dwell on the earth?" have hope (Revelation 6:10). Don't despair in the day of adversity!

The night will be very dark, *but* joy comes in the morning. Remember that, and don't faint.

Believe God, and live accordingly.

Determine to know your God and His Word intimately.

Take time to study God's Word, to be still and know that He is God.

Though others turn to their own ways, their own solutions, you live as the redeemed should live...for your redemption and your Redeemer draw nigh.

> *"And not only this but we also exult in our tribulations, knowing that tribulation brings about perseverance; and perseverance, proven character; and proven character, hope; and hope does not disappoint, because the love of God has been poured out within our hearts through the Holy Spirit who was given to us"* (Romans 5:3-5).

MY RESPONSE TO HIS WORDS...

My Response to His Words...

When You're Concerned for a Loved One

Have you prayed and prayed about something, yet God hasn't answered?

Maybe you've been agonizing over a son or daughter, your husband or wife, or even a grandchild. Or maybe you've been asking God to deliver you from a stressful situation or to meet some need...and nothing has happened.

Are you worn out and ready to give up, ready to throw in the towel and call it quits because you think your prayer will never be answered?

What do you do when you look around at your situation and nothing has changed? When you're asking God for things that circumstantially look absolutely impossible?

What do you do when you become weary in prayer, despairing of ever seeing God answer?

Do you give up? Write God off as being deaf, uncaring, or not true to His Word?

Oh, Beloved, don't write God off. Don't quit. Don't lose hope.

In Luke 11:1-13 Jesus tells us to persist until we see the answer. We are to keep on asking until it's given to us. We're to keep on seeking until we find it. We are to keep on knocking until the door is opened.

Ask, seek, and knock are all present-tense verbs here in the original Greek, which means that they speak of continuous or habitual action. Therefore, if we believe Jesus means what He says, we'll do what He tells us to do.

One of the major keys to answered prayer is *persistence*.

When the disciples asked Jesus to teach them to pray, Jesus gave them what we call "The Lord's Prayer," which in actuality is *a way* to pray (Luke 11:2-4; see also Matthew 6:9-13). After giving them this pattern for prayer, Jesus said to them,

> *"Suppose one of you has a friend, and goes to him at midnight and says to him, 'Friend, lend me three loaves; for a friend of mine has come to me from a journey, and I have nothing to set before him'; and from inside he answers and says, 'Do not bother me; the door has already been shut and my children and I are in bed; I cannot get up and give you anything.' I tell you, even though he will not get up and give him anything because he is his friend, yet because of his persistence he will get up and give him as much as he needs"* (Luke 11:5-8).

Later, Jesus told His disciples "a parable to show that at all times they ought to pray and not to lose heart" (Luke 18:1).

Isn't this where we often fail? It's easier to quit than to persist…easier to throw up our hands in defeat than to hold on in faith, not letting go until we receive what we're asking for.

The problem is, we're an impatient people. We don't like to wait. When our prayers are not answered right away, then we're eager to take things into our own hands and try to do what, in reality, only God can do. And when we get impatient and do it our way, we mess up!

If there is a delay in the answer, you can be sure it's because God has a *purpose*. His ways are not our ways. His timetable is not the same as ours.

For forty years Bill Bright prayed every single day, asking God to open Russia for the gospel. He persisted. He never stopped. The discouraging news from Russia and about Russia under Communist rule never hindered Bill's prayers. Then, the Iron Curtain came down. After forty years of prayer, Bill was given the awesome opportunity to preach to thousands in Moscow.

Mia and Costel Oglice, our Romanian staff couple who serve as our Eurasian Ministry Directors for Precept Ministries International, began praying more than thirty years ago, asking God to do the seemingly impossible. While living in Romania under the dark and oppressive rule of Ceausescu, they felt led to pray what seemed to be a ridiculous prayer: that the gospel would be preached in the stadiums of Romania and across the country on radio and television.

How could something like this ever be possible? The way things were, it would cost the people their freedom or even their lives if they attended a Bible study or shared the Word of God with another. Yet Mia and Costel persisted in prayer year after year.

And look what happened! Mia and Costel themselves now speak over radio and television in Romania.

For years my husband and I cried out to God for our oldest son, Tom. This was my "hidden" heartache. Tommy was a "beloved adversary" who tried to discredit my name, my God, and His calling upon my life.

Over and over I beseeched God on behalf of my firstborn. I bent over backwards trying to please him. And I did all I could do to turn him around. But nothing worked. Plus, on top of it all, I had to deal with envy as I watched other mothers whose sons loved the Lord. At other times I rehearsed my own failures over and over until I was exhausted. Then I'd run back and cling to His promise in Romans 8:28-30.

Then, one day, God said, "Be still, Kay. Cease striving. Let go. Relax and know that I am God."

So I shut up and quit trying to straighten Tommy out. I just started listening and loving him unconditionally and persisting in prayer. As a matter of fact, I think my prayers became more fervent, because I was shut up to nothing but God. What intimacy this brings—what dependence!

God had me right where He wanted me to be—right where I needed to be.

Then in 1993, Jesus set our 37-year-old son free from a lifetime of immorality and gave him a passionate love for God the Father, for God's Word, and for God's people...and, hallelujah, for his mama! My joy knows no bounds! I stand in awe, and so do others, at the miracle of it all, for God has truly transformed our son.

Try as we might, we cannot change another person's heart. Only God can. God alone is our hope, our refuge, our very present help in the time of need and trouble. When will we learn to simply do what God says:

- to pray and not faint,

- to persist and not quit,

- to trust Him,

- to wait upon Him until He brings it to pass?

Believe me, I know the process is hard, but if you're convinced by His Spirit that what you're asking for is in accord with His Word, His will, and His character (John 15:7; 1 John 5:14; John 16:24) and you're not asking merely to satisfy your own desires (James 4:2-3), then persist.

Don't give God rest until you see His answer.

Though He "slays" you, trust Him.

Though the answer to your prayer tarries—even for years—it will come.

So cease striving. Let go. Relax. Wait upon God who alone accomplishes great things which we know not.

You may not see it, but He is at work.

> *"I say to you, ask, and it will be given to you; seek, and you will find; knock, and it will be opened to you. For everyone who asks, receives; and he who seeks, finds; and to him who knocks, it will be opened" (Luke 11:9-10).*

MY RESPONSE TO HIS WORDS...

My Response to His Words...

When You Feel
Like a Failure

Are you seeing things God's way?

Are you discontented? Unhappy?

Maybe, just maybe, it's because your thinking has been colored by the world!

Maybe, just maybe, it's because you are off truth's center and, therefore, you're not able to see things from God's perspective.

If you could see things His way, then your unhappiness would fade and your discontentment would turn to joy. Because you would have His evaluation of the situation, and you would see that you aren't a failure. Instead, you would realize that it's all part of His bigger purpose.

Yesterday as I walked and prayed and examined my dreams and desires in the light of the Word of God, I realized how influenced we are by the movies and television programs we've seen, by the books and magazines we've read, by the teachers and peers we've listened to and observed (some with envy), and by the songs we've sung until their words have been lodged deep in our hearts.

And then, of course, many of the world's ways, songs, values, and philosophies have been taken up by the church and integrated into its worship, counsel, thinking, teaching, writing, and programming (including religious television). So there has been that added exposure and indoctrination.

If we have had a steady diet of these things and have not had equal or greater time in the Bible itself, then is it any wonder that the world has squeezed us into its mold? And is it any wonder that we don't even recognize it?

I believe this kind of exposure is one of the reasons—a major reason—that our Christianity has had, and is having, such a diminishing influence on our society today. I believe this indoctrination is why our nation, our future—and even the church—are in such jeopardy.

Let me give you a small sampling of where we are off truth's center if we embrace such thoughts.

OUR THINKING SAYS: A close-knit, happy family is evidence that I am blessed of God and have raised my children properly.
GOD'S WORD SAYS:

> *"Do you suppose that I came to grant peace on earth? I tell you, no, but rather division; for from now on five members in one household will be divided, three against two, and two against three. They will be divided, father against son and son against father, mother against daughter and daughter against mother, mother-in-law against daughter-in-law and daughter-in-law against mother-in-law"* (Luke 12:51-53).

OUR THINKING SAYS: Things will make me happy. Besides, having things in abundance proves I am fulfilled, successful, and blessed.
GOD'S WORD SAYS:

> *"Beware, and be on your guard against every form of greed; for not even when one has an abundance does his life consist of his possessions"* (Luke 12:15).

OUR THINKING SAYS: I can't do that for my Lord; my first obligation is to my family.

GOD'S WORD SAYS:

> *"Peter said, 'Behold, we have left our own homes and followed You.' And He said to them, 'Truly I say to you, there is no one who has left house or wife or brothers or parents or children, for the sake of the kingdom of God, who will not receive many times as much at this time and in the age to come, eternal life"* (Luke 18:28-30).

OUR THINKING SAYS: God does not expect us, His people, to suffer.

GOD'S WORD SAYS:

> *"Beloved, do not be surprised at the fiery ordeal among you, which comes upon you for your testing, as though some strange thing were happening to you; but to the degree that you share the sufferings of Christ, keep on rejoicing, so that also at the revelation of His glory you may rejoice with exultation. If you are reviled for the name of Christ, you are blessed, because the Spirit of glory and of God rests on you"* (1 Peter 4:12-14).

OUR THINKING SAYS: God has given me an abundance so I can have financial security and more things. Bigger houses, more houses, more clothes, more, more, more.

GOD'S WORD SAYS:

> *"He told them a parable, saying, 'The land of a rich man was very productive. And he began reasoning to himself, saying, "What shall I do, since I have no place to store my crops?" Then he said, "This is what I will do; I will tear down my barns and build larger ones, and there I will store all my grain and my goods. And I will say to my soul, 'Soul, you have many goods laid up for many years to come; take your ease, eat, drink and be merry.'" But God said to him, "You fool! This very night your soul is required of you; and now who will own what you have prepared?" So is the man who stores up treasure for himself, and is not rich toward God'"* (Luke 12:16-21).

OUR THINKING SAYS: My mate is not meeting my needs. I can seek love and a better relationship elsewhere.
GOD'S WORD SAYS:

> *"Marriage is to be held in honor among all, and the marriage bed is to be undefiled; for fornicators and adulterers God will judge" (Hebrews 13:4).*

OUR THINKING SAYS: Because God loves me, He won't allow me to suffer.
GOD'S WORD SAYS:

> *"Who will separate us from the love of Christ? Will tribulation, or distress, or persecution, or famine, or nakedness, or peril, or sword? Just as it is written, 'For Your sake we are being put to death all day long; we were considered as sheep to be slaughtered.' But in all these things we overwhelmingly conquer through Him who loved us" (Romans 8:35-37).*

OUR THINKING SAYS: If certain things came into my life, I know I couldn't handle them.
GOD'S WORD SAYS:

> *"No temptation has overtaken you but such as is common to man; and God is faithful, who will not allow you to be tempted beyond what you are able, but with the temptation will provide the way of escape also, so that you will be able to endure it" (1 Corinthians 10:13).*

> *"I can do all things through Him who strengthens me" (Philippians 4:13).*

OUR THINKING SAYS: Those poor people. What tragic lives they've had. They will never recover. It will ruin them forever.
GOD'S WORD SAYS:

> *"We know that God causes all things to work together for good to those who love God, to those who are called according to His purpose. For those whom He foreknew, He also predestined to become conformed to the image of His Son, so that He would be the firstborn*

*among many brethren; and these whom He predestined,
He also called; and these whom He called, He also jus-
tified; and these whom He justified, He also glorified"*
(Romans 8:28-30).

OUR THINKING SAYS: God wouldn't want me, couldn't use me, won't accept me—I'm nothing.

GOD'S WORD SAYS:

*"Consider your calling, brethren, that there were not
many wise according to the flesh, not many mighty, not
many noble; but God has chosen the foolish things of the
world to shame the wise, and God has chosen the weak
things of the world to shame the things which are
strong, and the base things of the world and the
despised God has chosen, the things that are not, so
that He may nullify the things that are, so that no man
may boast before God. But by His doing you are in
Christ Jesus, who became to us wisdom from God, and
righteousness and sanctification, and redemption, so
that, just as it is written, 'Let him who boasts, boast in
the Lord'"* (1 Corinthians 1:26-31).

OUR THINKING SAYS: If our kids are going to make it in this world, they've got to be educated by the world.

GOD'S WORD SAYS:

*"It is written, 'I will destroy the wisdom of the wise,
and the cleverness of the clever I will set aside.' Where
is the wise man? Where is the scribe? Where is the
debater of this age? Has not God made foolish the
wisdom of the world?"* (1 Corinthians 1:19-20).

OUR THINKING SAYS: Now that I'm saved, I'm safe and on my way to heaven. I can live any way I want.

GOD'S WORD SAYS:

*"Every tree that does not bear good fruit is cut down and
thrown into the fire"* (Matthew 7:19).

I could go on and on, but I am sure you get the point.

If your thinking is not going to be colored by the world, then you must be transformed by the renewing of your mind. And the only way to renew your mind is to get into the Word of God and meditate upon it day in and day out.

Esteem God's Word as more precious than your necessary food—because it is. It is your bread of life...it is the light for your path...it is the place where you can rest in peace and contentment.

> *"Do not be conformed to this world, but be transformed by the renewing of your mind, so that you may prove what the will of God is, that which is good and acceptable and perfect" (Romans 12:2).*

My Response to His Words...

When People
Ask for Your Advice

*Have you, as a Christian, ever counseled
another Christian regarding a problem?*

Have you ever counseled another Christian regarding whether they should take some specific action?

And what kind of counsel did you give them, Beloved?

In the book of Malachi, we find that God addresses this very matter.

In the days of the prophet Malachi, God was calling His people to return to Him. They had done a number of things that had displeased Him, and thus He withheld His hand of blessing, and their intimacy with Him dulled.

One of those displeasing things was that the priests were not giving God's people the right instruction.

Speaking of the priest Levi, God said,

> *"True instruction was in his mouth and unrighteousness was not found on his lips; he walked with Me in peace and uprightness, and he turned many back from*

iniquity. For the lips of a priest should preserve knowl-edge, and men should seek instruction from his mouth; for he is the messenger of the LORD of hosts" (Malachi 2:6-7).

But of the priests He was rebuking in Malachi's day, God said,

" 'As for you, you have turned aside from the way; you have caused many to stumble by the instruction; you have corrupted the covenant of Levi,' says the LORD of hosts, '…just as you are not keeping My ways but are showing partiality in the instruction' " (Malachi 2:8-9).

It is an awesome thing to speak for God or to counsel God's child! This is why God gives the warning He does in James 3:1:

"Let not many of you become teachers, my brethren, knowing that as such we will incur a stricter judgment."

It is part of the nature of man to want someone else to tell him what to do, for then the need for making a decision is off his shoulders. If something should go wrong, he can always blame it on someone else! (This nature of sin goes right back to the Garden of Eden—where Adam blamed Eve, and Eve blamed the serpent.)

Also, many times when people seek counsel from another, they are actually seeking to confirm their own desires. If the counsel they are given concurs with what they want to do anyway, they take it as a confirmation.

Is all counseling wrong, then? Should one Christian not seek counsel from another?

No, counsel is fine. In fact, the book of Proverbs teaches,

"In abundance of counselors there is victory" (Proverbs 11:14).

No, receiving counsel is not wrong. The problem does not lie in seeking counsel. The warning is directed to the person giving the counsel or instruction. The primary responsibility rests upon the shoulders of the counselor—a weighty responsibility indeed.

If you should ever advise another, you must make sure that what you give is "true instruction." By "true instruction" God means that which is in accordance with the *whole* counsel of God's Word.

If you give counsel that contradicts God's Word, then unrighteousness is on your lips and you could cause other people to turn aside from God's will for their lives.

How careful we need to be as "kings and priests unto God and his Father" (Revelation 1:6 KJV) not to show partiality to the person or to their circumstances when we give them counsel, but to say...

> *"As the LORD lives, what my God says, that I will speak" (2 Chronicles 18:13).*

MY RESPONSE TO HIS WORDS...

My Response to His Words...

When You Question God's Faithfulness

When we fail God,
what does He do?

Does He take back all His promises and walk away?

As we read through the Old Testament, it sometimes seems that no one failed God more than Israel.

They had broken every commandment.

They had challenged His love for them.

They had despised and defiled His name.

They had wearied Him with their tolerance of evil.

They had robbed Him of His rightful tithes and offerings.

They had even spoken against Him, saying that it was vain to serve Him.

Oh, there were some among them who had not been partakers of this rebellion. There were

> *"those who feared the LORD...and the LORD gave attention and heard it, and a book of remembrance was written before Him for those who fear the LORD and who esteem His name" (Malachi 3:16).*

Yes, God took note of this faithful remnant and said,

> *"They will be Mine...on the day that I prepare My own possession, and I will spare them as a man spares his own son who serves him"* (Malachi 3:17).

God would not fail or forsake the righteous nor would He go back on His covenant with Israel.

And so, before He became silent for 400 years, He gave them His promise—a magnificent, glorious, immutable promise:

> *"Behold, I am going to send My messenger, and he will clear the way before Me. And the Lord, whom you seek, will suddenly come to His temple; and the messenger of the covenant, in whom you delight, behold, He is coming"* (Malachi 3:1).

God was confirming the promise of the coming of Messiah (Christ) and His forerunner. Finally, the promise of the new covenant proclaimed by the prophet Jeremiah would be fulfilled:

> *"'Behold, days are coming,' declares the LORD, 'when I will make a new covenant with the house of Israel and with the house of Judah, not like the covenant which I made with their fathers in the day I took them by the hand to bring them out of the land of Egypt, My covenant which they broke....But this is the covenant which I will make with the house of Israel after those days....I will put My law within them and on their heart I will write it; and I will be their God, and they shall be My people...for I will forgive their iniquity, and their sin I will remember no more'"* (Jeremiah 31:31-34).

The One appointed...

> *"as a covenant to the people, as a light to the nations, to open blind eyes, to bring out prisoners from the dungeon and those who dwell in darkness from the prison"* (Isaiah 42:6-7)

...was coming!

This was their sure promise from God! His final promise to which they were to cling during the years of silence that would follow!

Israel waited through 400 years of silence for the fulfillment of God's last promise in Malachi, but it did come to pass. It had to, for God had promised.

How similar it is to our promise as the church of Jesus Christ.

For as the Old Testament closed with the promise of the coming of Messiah, so our New Testament closes with the promise of the second coming of Christ.

We have been waiting almost 2,000 years, but we have His promise—even when He is silent.

> *"Behold, I am coming quickly, and My reward is with Me, to render to every man according to what he has done. I am the Alpha and the Omega, the first and the last, the beginning and the end....Yes, I am coming quickly" (Revelation 22:12-13,20).*

MY RESPONSE TO HIS WORDS...

My Response to His Words...

When People Need Love and Understanding

Do you long to have someone take you by the hand and show you how to survive the traumas of life?

Someone to talk to. Someone to listen. Someone who won't walk away no matter what you say. Someone to care...to love you unconditionally.

That is what you need...what I need...what we all need, isn't it?

The Lord is the Someone who is always there...always ready to listen, to guide. But He has also called all believers to be part of His visible body here on earth, which offers us the awesome, yet wonderful opportunity of being that someone who reaches out to others.

How well this truth has been brought home to me through Precept Ministries.

I think of a letter I received from a young man thanking me for sending him our Precept Bible study course on Philippians, *How to Have Joy No Matter What!*

He began by saying, "I want to tell you something that I have never told to anyone. It's something so horrible that happened to me at the age of nine and I cannot get it out of my mind. In fact it seems to get worse as I cannot stop thinking about it."

As I read his story, written from his prison cell, I could tell just from the way it was written that even putting the words on paper had been excruciatingly painful for him.

As he sought to tell me what his parents had done to him, there were some words he couldn't even write; he used dashes instead, because it was just too horrible for him to even write it.

When this young man was only nine years old, he walked into his parents' bedroom one evening. He was lonely. He knew his parents didn't love him, but he had not given up hope. The bedroom door, which they had shut early in the evening, left him an orphan in his own home, but he would not be deterred by it. He would try again.

When he walked in, his parents were looking at child pornography. Horrified, never having seen anything like this before, the child turned to walk out. His parents ordered him to stay. He sat there, stone still, as they looked at the pictures and discussed which things they should try. The loneliness created by that closed door was now something he longed for.

That night, already deprived of natural affection, that nine-year-old child was raped of innocence as he became a victim of his parents' sexual perversion. At the age of twelve he ran away from their home.

Now, as a young man, he was writing to us, telling how desperately he wants to learn how to have joy no matter what!

Is it possible? Many would say "No!" And if it weren't for God, I would say the same.

But God is our Jehovah-rapha, the Lord who heals. And God has a body...the church. And God has a book...the Bible. And when members of His body take His book and live by it and minister through it, there is healing. And with the healing comes joy.

What this young man needs is someone to listen, to care, to share with him the truths of God's Word so that he can deal with the traumas of his past. Someone to come alongside him as Jesus would if He dwelt upon this earth.

When I think of the body reaching out, I also think of an evening I spent at one of our summer Teen Boot Camps. At that camp they were studying *Lord, Heal My Hurts,* and on the last night, we had a sharing time. It began at 10:00 P.M. and went, unexpectedly, until 2:45 A.M. We prayed, cried, sang...as teen after teen shared their experiences with the traumas of divorce, rejection, loneliness, and of the devastation that alcohol had caused in their lives—some because they were the abuser, some because their parents were the abusers.

What vivid contrasts were evident that night as we listened to teens who came from godly homes and who had walked with the Lord and then to those who had not come from such homes.

As one young man started sobbing because "my dad loves his drugs more than he loves me," another young man jumped up and came and put his arms around him, saying, "I want to pray for you."

Then, at about 2:00 A.M., a young man, unsaved but listening carefully to everything that was being taught, came up and took the microphone. It was obvious that he was hurting when he said, "I'm only sixteen, and I am a father. My parents don't even know they have a two-month-old granddaughter."

He wasn't ready to receive Jesus yet, but he asked for prayer. He didn't want his little girl to get messed up like he had—the daughter whose life he had spared when he convinced his girlfriend not to have an abortion.

I wish you could have been in the center of that prayer huddle with us and heard the prayers of those teenagers for that little girl's spiritual health and for that young father's salvation. We wept and prayed for about thirty minutes...and this young man knew God's people cared.

How desperately we need to understand our place in the body, to accept our responsibility to be God's someone in the life of one of His children.

That is what we are all about at Precept Ministries—teaching and training God's people, the church, to minister according to God's Word. Our goal is not just knowledge, but life...lived His way for His glory; reaching out with His love, His counsel, His wisdom to those who need someone to help them live as more than conquerors.

If you are ministering in a prison, you may meet the man whose life took its cruel twist through parents who didn't know God. Do more than preach to him...be God's someone.

If teens hang around your house, they are your opportunity for ministry. Listen to them, love them, model for them what Christianity is all about. You could be God's someone for their salvation, for their future.

If you are His child, you have one or more spiritual gifts given to you by God for the edification of that body of believers. Ask God to show you what gifts are yours, and then get busy.

This is what Christianity is all about—Jesus living in you and making you an extension of His hands, arms, feet. See with His eyes. Listen with His ears. Speak His words.

Be God's someone.

> *"As each one has received a special gift, employ it in serving one another as good stewards of the manifold grace of God. Whoever speaks is to do so as one who is speaking the utterances of God; whoever serves is to do so as one who is serving by the strength which God supplies; so that in all things God may be glorified through Jesus Christ, to whom belongs the glory and dominion forever and ever. Amen" (1 Peter 4:10-11).*

My Response to His Words...

When You Wonder
If Jesus Will Ever Come

---

*If you really believed that the
second coming of our Lord was
imminent, would it affect the way
you celebrate His first coming?*

Every December for more than 2,000 years men and women
have looked back incredulously to the day that saw a 4,000-year-
old prophecy fulfilled as God burst forth from Mary's womb.

Ordained the Lamb that would take away the sins of the world,
there He was—God, clothed with the flesh of mankind.

No wonder the angels sang!

The Christ had come, heralding the beginning of "the last
days"—the last days, in which the prince of this world would be cast
out...the last days, which would bring to an end the heavenly conflict between God and Satan (Revelation 12).

How could the angels not rejoice?

Yet as the heavenly host alerted the shepherds in Bethlehem to
the birth of their King, most of mankind slept.

For thirty-three years Jesus lived among those He came to
save. And for the last three of those years He performed signs and

wonders, providing irrefutable testimony that He was the Christ, the Son of God.

Before mankind's very eyes, 333 prophecies were in the process of being fulfilled, one by one and over and over again.

They shouldn't have missed what was happening. Yet most were ignorant of the Word of God, and, therefore, unaware of what was unfolding before their eyes. Tragically they did not recognize the time of His visitation.

Is it any wonder Jesus wept openly as He entered Jerusalem for the last time? There He was—the unmistakable fulfillment of Zechariah's prophecy—and they knew Him not. Listen:

> *"As soon as He was approaching, near the descent of the Mount of Olives, the whole crowd of the disciples began to praise God joyfully with a loud voice for all the miracles which they had seen, shouting, 'Blessed is the King who comes in the name of the Lord; peace in heaven and glory in the highest!' Some of the Pharisees in the crowd said to Him, 'Teacher, rebuke Your disciples.' But Jesus answered, 'I tell you, if these become silent, the stones will cry out!'*
>
> *"When He approached Jerusalem, He saw the city and wept over it, saying, 'If you had known in this day, even you, the things which make for peace! But now they have been hidden from your eyes. For the days will come upon you when your enemies will throw up a barricade against you, and surround you and hem you in on every side, and will level you to the ground and your children within you, and they will not leave in you one stone upon another, because you did not recognize the time of your visitation'"* (Luke 19:37-44).

This prophecy was fulfilled only a few decades later, in A.D. 70, when Titus, the Roman general, destroyed Jerusalem, killing more than one million Jews.

Luke 19 is loaded with prophetic import, and if the Jews of Jesus' day had known their own Scriptures—for example, Daniel 9:24-27—they would have recognized that what He was saying and doing, at that moment, proved that He was who He said He was.

Sadly, I cannot help but see a parallel to our times.

Today, as in Jesus' day, many are asleep. They don't recognize the nearness of our Lord's second and final visitation. As a result, His temple is desolate of His Shekinah glory, and our nation, our world, is about to be destroyed. Yet multitudes—even in the church—are totally ignorant of the significance of the events escalating daily in our world which point to the imminent return of our Lord.

The strengthening of the European Union, the conflict in the Middle East, the proposed rebuilding of Babylon, the Jews' determination to rebuild the temple, and the preparation of the temple vessels by the Jews herald the fact that His second coming draws near.

As the time of His second visitation breaks upon the horizon, we need to set the alarm on God's time clock. We must not be caught sleeping.

Remember that what you are today, that what you do today, will not go unrewarded or unchallenged by the Lord. If you are His, you're not your own. You're a steward—a steward of all that's given to you at salvation—and stewards must give an account.

How should you live so you won't be ashamed when you see Him face-to-face?

Get alone with Him, take pen and paper, and ask your heavenly Father that very question. Honestly deal with those things that would keep you from looking unashamedly into His face. Then live accordingly.

Never since our Lord walked on planet Earth has there been such a rapid turn of prophetic events as those we now see occurring. Those who know His Word and understand His prophecies realize that these are significant days.

I wonder if our Lord weeps in heaven because many, like those 2,000 years ago, are not aware that the stage is almost set for His return as King of kings and Lord of lords.

> *"Let a man regard us in this manner, as servants of Christ and stewards of the mysteries of God"* *(1 Corinthians 4:1).*

MY RESPONSE TO HIS WORDS...

My Response to His Words...

When You're Tempted to Please Others

What will matter in eternity?

Someday soon this earthly life is all going to be over! And what will matter then?

How smart, capable, or successful we were? How loved, appreciated, or applauded we were? How much we possessed? How much we achieved? How much we accomplished?

Will it matter whether we were attractive or ugly, smart or dumb, sick or poor, known or unknown?

No!

When this earthly life is over, when all is said and done, none of these things—which now seem so important—will matter.

Only one thing will matter on "that day"—the same thing that mattered to Jesus when His thirty-three years on earth came to a close.

When His life on this earth was over, Jesus could honestly say,

> *"I glorified You on the earth, having accomplished the work which You have given Me to do" (John 17:4).*

When "the day of the Lord" comes (and I think it will come sooner than we think), the only thing that will matter is that you and I have glorified Him on earth and have finished the work that He has given us to do individually.

To glorify Him means to live in such a way that our lives truly demonstrate who He is.

One of my weaknesses is seeking to please people—trying to keep everyone happy—and I have to remember that it is God whom I have to serve. He alone must be my God! If not, I'm not demonstrating who He truly is!

Am I—are we—doing what He has called us to do, to be? Or are we trying to fulfill the expectations of others?

God is our director—*and our audience. We only have to please Him.*

Jesus could say what He said in John 17:4 because He always and only pleased the Father—not Himself, not His family, not His friends, not His associates, not the crowd.

The question comes to us, then: "How am I going to know what pleases Him?"

His answer is simple…and yet not so simple.

Simple in that we'll know His will if we learn to meet with Him each day and listen to His Word.

First we must be in His book—the Bible.

Second, we must seek and ask His direction; then we must be still so that we can hear His still, small voice which tells us, "This is the way…walk in it."

Jesus' habit was to get alone with the Father. And this is where the answer to "How am I going to know what pleases Him?" is not so simple.

There's so much noise, so much pressure—there are so many people pulling on us—that being alone and quiet can be a major battle.

But the battle must be won. If it's not, then the wrong things will matter, and we won't be able to say we have glorified Him on earth and have finished the work He's given us to do. When that happens, our lives will be lived at man's direction, and we'll never satisfy our human audience.

Therefore, let's give Him thanks and do whatever is necessary to live according to His will and direction.

Nothing else really matters!
We are accountable only to an audience of One.

> *"Teach me Your way, O LORD;*
> *I will walk in Your truth;*
> *Unite my heart to fear Your name.*
> *I will give thanks to You, O Lord my God,*
>   *with all my heart,*
> *And will glorify Your name forever" (Psalm*
>   *86:11-12).*

MY RESPONSE TO HIS WORDS...

My Response to His Words...

When Your Faith Is Tested

Do you really trust God in all things?
Are you clinging to His sufficiency?

The trial has come...the test of your faith.
Will you believe?
Will you cling to God?
Will you walk by faith?
Will you say, "Though He slay me, yet will I trust Him?"
God, and God alone, holds your life and well-being in His hands. Perhaps you believe that most of the time, but...
Are there any "buts" when, in any and every situation of life, the only One who can turn the tide is God?
No! He alone is sufficient!
Our help comes from the One who made the heavens and the earth—the One who loves us with an everlasting love.

> *"Blessed is the man who trusts in the LORD and whose trust is the LORD. For he will be like a tree planted by the water, that extends its roots by a stream and will not fear when the heat comes; but its leaves will be green, and it will not be anxious in a year of drought nor cease to yield fruit"* (Jeremiah 17:7-8).

Indeed, we—you and I—can have green leaves in drought time. In drought time we can bear fruit.

"Shall we indeed accept good from God and not accept adversity?" (Job 2:10).

In acceptance lies peace.

Not in resignation, but in acceptance. When you cast yourself on Him and do all you can by acting responsibly in regard to all God's leading and nothing changes, God is still there on His throne—and He is adequate.

His character has not changed. His name remains the same, and so do the promises of His Word.

Our responsibility is to cling, to believe. He is Jehovah-jireh, the Lord who will provide all our needs.

God, and God alone, is sufficient. He is able.

How I wish you and I could sit down together so I could share with you some of the letters I receive. Like me, you'd be heartbroken over the pain many have and are enduring. But you'd be so awed and encouraged at what God does when individuals decide to believe Him.

The Word of God has the answers. It is the answer to every circumstance of life.

So although we can't sit down together, I'd like to share portions of two letters, which I believe will encourage you...and at the same time speak to your heart.

Some time ago a woman wrote to us for help. She had left her first husband, become a transsexual, had a radical mastectomy, taken male hormones, and then married a woman. When she wrote to us, she told how she had finally realized how horribly she had sinned against God. I wrote back, shared Scripture God had given me for her, and sent a book and tapes.

Well, God did a miracle. The woman called her former husband and his parents and begged their forgiveness. She went back to being a woman, and her marriage to the woman was dissolved. Let me share part of what the woman's mother wrote to me.

As the mother of a transsexual, I want to thank you for writing her. After being rejected by ministers and ministries, the hurts were so bad, plus the self-condemnation and regrets, I was afraid she would give up. God is so good! Your letter was timed by God. When she received it she called me and just sobbed "someone besides you and God cares for me and wants to help me." We let happy tears flow.

I cried out for help too, as the mother of a transsexual, and wrote to a couple of men of God whom I felt would help me. Even my prayer partner never mentioned it to me after I confided in her. I think I understand why the silence. They didn't know or understand either. I think it would have helped so much to have had a support group but evidently God wanted me to go through this experience alone with Him. If I can help any other mother with this terrible pain, I would be more than happy to.

God, and God alone, has done a miracle.

In that regard, there is another letter I would like to share with you.

Let me begin by saying that I was abused verbally and sexually for at least ten years while growing up. Later, I was into prostitution, drug and alcohol abuse, and a multitude of other sins. I've had two abortions, and the list goes on and on....But, all praise to God. I'll boast in Him! He and He alone has healed me. My deep pain is gone. My bitterness is gone. My bondage to sin is gone. God changed, not only the outward sins, but also inner sin.

Only God and I know how perverted and distorted my thoughts were and how He has transformed my mind into a joyful, God-centered, sound mind....Others sent me to counselor after counselor until people virtually gave up hope. But then, by God's grace, I decided to believe God's Word, and as I believed God, I obeyed Him. God showed me I was free to choose (unlike psychology which said I was doomed because of my past). I began to renew my mind in His Word. I accepted His sovereign will in placing me in my "messed up" family. He gave me a promise (2 Corinthians 1:3-11) that He

*would eventually use everything for good....Though the
natural man cannot understand it (God's ways are not
our ways), God's way works! Simple faith and acting on
God's Word has healed me....May God open our eyes
to see Him as our only Healer!*

God and God alone deserves all the glory. He has brought all that
you've read in these letters to pass because these dear people heard
the truth, the Word of God, and decided to make the Lord their trust
and to trust in the Lord. And green leaves and fruit sprang forth even
in drought time!

He freed me, He freed my firstborn....He can free you, for He
came to set the captive free.

Cry out to Him, Beloved—He will heal...and you will be free!

*"Heal me, O LORD, and I will be healed; save me and
I will be saved, for You are my praise"* (Jeremiah
17:14).

"If the Son makes you free, you will be free indeed"
(John 8:36).

*"You will know the truth, and the truth will make you
free"* (John 8:32).

My Response to His Words...

Harvest House Books
by Kay Arthur

∿∿∿∿

Beloved
God, Are You There?
His Imprint, My Expression
How to Study Your Bible
Israel, My Beloved
Just a Moment with You, God
Lord, Teach Me to Pray in 28 Days
A Marriage Without Regrets
A Marriage Without Regrets Study Guide
With an Everlasting Love

Bibles
The New Inductive Study Bible (NASB)

Discover 4 Yourself
Inductive Bible Studies for Kids
How to Study Your Bible for Kids
Lord, Teach Me to Pray for Kids
God's Amazing Creation (Genesis 1–2)
Digging Up the Past (Genesis 3–11)
Abraham—God's Brave Explorer (Genesis 11–25)
Joseph—God's Superhero (Genesis 37–50)
Wrong Way, Jonah! (Jonah)
Jesus in the Spotlight (John 1–11)
Jesus—Awesome Power, Awesome Love (John 11–16)
Jesus—To Eternity and Beyond! (John 17–21)
Boy, Have I Got Problems! (James)
God, What's Your Name

BOOKS IN THE
NEW INDUCTIVE STUDY SERIES

~~~~

Teach Me Your Ways
Genesis, Exodus,
Leviticus, Numbers,
Deuteronomy

*Choosing Victory,
Overcoming Defeat*
Joshua, Judges, Ruth

Desiring God's Own Heart
1 & 2 Samuel,
1 Chronicles

Walking Faithfully with God
1 & 2 Kings, 2 Chronicles

*Overcoming Fear
and Discouragement*
Ezra, Nehemiah, Esther

*Trusting God
in Times of Adversity*
Job

*God's Blueprint for
Bible Prophecy*
Daniel

*Opening the Windows
of Blessings*
Haggai, Zechariah,
Malachi

The Call to Follow Jesus
Luke

*The Holy Spirit
Unleashed in You*
Acts

*Experiencing the Real
Power of Faith*
Romans

*God's Answers for
Relationships and Passions*
1 & 2 Corinthians

*Free from Bondage
God's Way*
Galatians, Ephesians

That I May Know Him
Philippians, Colossians

*Standing Firm in
These Last Days*
1 & 2 Thessalonians

*Walking in Power,
Love, and Discipline*
1 & 2 Timothy, Titus

*Living with Discernment
in the End Times*
1 & 2 Peter, Jude

Behold, Jesus Is Coming!
Revelation